Dream Windows

Dream Windows

An Inspirational Guide to Draperies and Soft Furnishings

CHARLES T. RANDALL
SHARON TEMPLETON

RANDALL INTERNATIONAL

Published in the United States by

Randall International
Orange, California

Distributed in Great Britain by

Antique Collectors Club Ltd
Woodbridge, Suffolk

First Edition

ISBN 1-890379-01-8

How to reach us:
Phone: (714) 771-8488
Toll Free: (800) 882-8907
Internet: http://www.randallonline.com
Illustrated by: Patricia M. Howard and Carlotta Tormey
Junior Editors: Hollie Wheeler and Joy Randall
Editor-in-Chief: Melanie Bysouth
Layout and Pre-Press Support: Jamey Wheeler and Elizabeth Randall
Cover Design by: Diego Linares
Pre-Press: 1st Global Graphics Inc., Irwindale, CA

Printed in China
Library of Congress Cataloging-in-Publication Data Upon Request

10 9 8 7 6 5 4 3 2 1

CONTENTS

INTRODUCTION

When striving for success, one must first strive for knowledge. And as one begins to learn about that which they desire, one becomes better prepared to obtain it.

To design a swag and cascade combination that will capture the attention of all who enter the room, one must first know what is needed to create the window treatment. When one aspires to understand the basics of design they become knowledgeable, efficient and confident and success will become inevitable.

Dream Windows can lead you to that success.

The format of each page is straightforward, easy-to-use and includes a basic overview describing the appearance and location of the treatment, complete calculations of fabric requirements including fabrics with pattern repeats, information the workroom needs so as to ensure accurate fabrication of the product and suggestions and notes that are unique to a specific product.

This book will be one of your most important decorating tools. The product pages provide the basis of all window treatments, as well as bedding and accessory options. The creative ways in which you, as a designer, combine treatments, details and fabrics, offer an infinite number of choices.

You will find the detailed illustrations to be an inspiring collection of finished work. And the "Designer's Sketchfile" will provide you with endless decorating possibilities-from simple curtains to extravagant puddled draperies from decorative trims to canopied four-poster beds.

And with a greater understanding of design, a successful window treatment will be yours.

NOTES ON CALCULATING YARDAGES

With drapery calculations, one must consider the following: width and length of window or area to be covered, amount of fullness desired, width of fabric to be used, allowances for hems, headings and styling and pattern repeat, if applicable. And after obtaining accurate measurements for each, proceed with the following steps.

Step 1) Determine the number of fabric widths required. This is calculated by multiplying the width of the window or area to be covered by the given fullness factor (listed on the item page). Divide this by the width of the fabric being used. The result is the number of widths of fabric that are required to achieve the desired fullness. Since fabric suppliers will not sell a part of the width, this figure must be a whole number.

Step 2a) Calculate the yardage. Add to the length of the window, or area to be covered, the allowances for hems, headings and, where applicable, styling allowances, such as for the pouf on a balloon shade- these allowances are listed on the item page under the corresponding yardage calculation. Next, multiply this amount by the number of widths required and divide by 36 to obtain the number of yards. This calculation applies only to solid fabrics or to fabrics that a have a pattern repeat of less than six inches.

OR (to calculate the yardage for a fabric with a pattern repeat of more than six inches)

Step 2b) Add the length and applicable allowances together and divide by the pattern repeat. This figure is the number of pattern repeats that are required to achieve the desired length. If this number is a fraction it must be rounded upward to the nearest whole number.

Step 2c) Determine the cut length- this is the actual length that the workroom will cut the fabric after allowing for pattern repeats, hems, etc. Multiply the number of repeats required by the size of the pattern repeat. This number is the cut length.

Step 2d) Multiply the number of widths required, as calculated in Step 1, by the cut length. Divide by 36 to obtain the total yardage required for a pattern repeat.

Note: Every attempt has been made to ensure the accuracy of the calculations and yardage charts of the items in this book. However, variations in fabrics or workroom specifications may require certain modifications to the yardage calculations. Please consult your workroom.

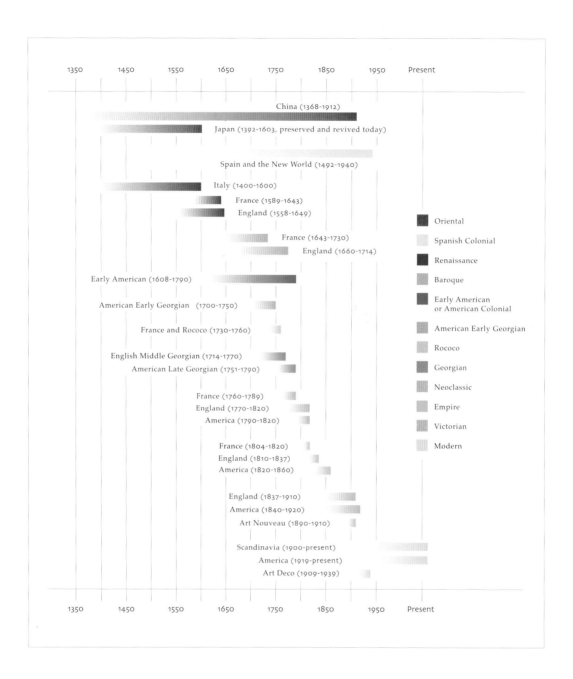

China (1368-1912)

Japan (1392-1603, preserved and revived today)

Spain and the New World (1492-1940)

Italy (1400-1600)

France (1589-1643)

England (1558-1649)

France (1643-1730)

England (1660-1714)

Early American (1608-1790)

American Early Georgian (1700-1750)

France and Rococo (1730-1760)

English Middle Georgian (1714-1770)

American Late Georgian (1751-1790)

France (1760-1789)

England (1770-1820)

America (1790-1820)

France (1804-1820)

England (1810-1837)

America (1820-1860)

England (1837-1910)

America (1840-1920)

Art Nouveau (1890-1910)

Scandinavia (1900-present)

America (1919-present)

Art Deco (1909-1939)

Oriental

Spanish Colonial

Renaissance

Baroque

Early American
or American Colonial

American Early Georgian

Rococo

Georgian

Neoclassic

Empire

Victorian

Modern

Overlapping Styles

The above chart represents the approximate dates of period styles as they relate to art, architecture and interior design. There was some overlapping of dates as styles changed in various regions at different times. For example, the Renaissance started in Italy but it took many years for the style of that period to reach England and France, by which time the Baroque Era had already begun in Italy.

THE RENAISSANCE 1440 - 1649

The recorded history of interior decoration starts with the Renaissance Era. It was during this time of great change and rebirth in the world of art and architecture that interior design became recognized as a specific art form. The concept of intentionally using one's interior furnishings as decoration, integrating fabrics in a unified and harmonious manner, gained popularity throughout Europe. The values and ideas of "civilized life indoors" began to follow a set of established principles. Thus began the art of interior design and the development of the window covering industry.

Wooden shutters were the primary style of window covering used during the Renaissance period. Mounted on either the interior or exterior of the house, shutters could

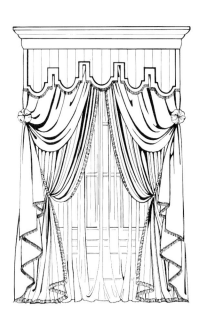

be closed over the window opening to protect from rain and block out strong sunlight, but did little to provide warmth. Shutters served a purely functional purpose.

The introduction of sheer fabrics allowed for simple, utilitarian curtain making during the sixteenth century. The curtains, most often made of a fine gauze or muslin, provided sun control and some degree of privacy. Hung from iron rods with hooks, usually in single panels, curtains did not become commonplace until after the 1650's.

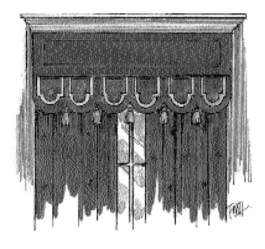

Although the decoration of windows during the Renaissance period was typically simple and understated, bed enclosures and partitions between rooms had curtains that were more elaborate. This allowed for privacy and prevented drafts and noises from traveling throughout the house. Curtains of this type were called "portiere", derived from the French word "porte" meaning door. The portiere would be hung "ensuite" (within the room). A panel of fabric, perhaps in silk, linen or wool, would be tied to one side during the day and pulled over the door at night for privacy.

During this era, the bed was a person's most cherished possession. Bedrooms of the nobility needed to reflect the importance of their owners. Four-poster beds with canopies were large wooden structures with elaborate

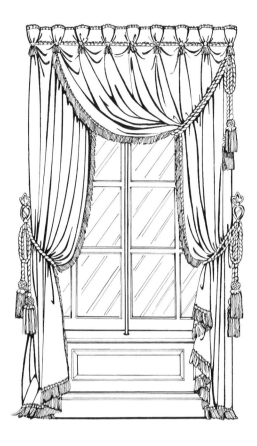

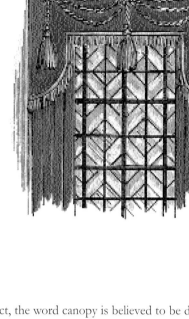

fact, the word canopy is believed to be derived from the Greek word "konops", meaning gnat.

Fabrics at this time were mostly plain weaves of silk, wool and cotton. As new weaving methods were developed, velvets and brocades in rich and vibrant colors became widely used throughout France and Italy. Cotton fabrics now had hand blocked prints and painted designs in large floral patterns.

hand carved motifs. Bed hangings were mounted under the canopies to close off the bed. In northern climates, this was to provide warmth and prevent drafts, whereas in the warmer Mediterranean countries, the primary function was to protect from mosquitoes and insects. In

Toward the end of the Renaissance, valances began to be incorporated into window treatments. Swags and pelmets, inspired by classical Greek motifs became the finishing touches to a more elaborate look that flourished during the Baroque era.

Baroque and Early Georgian 1643 - 1730

The Baroque period marked great developments in window dressing. For the first time in history, window curtains became a deliberate and distinctive decorative element to the interior design of a room. New advances in weaving techniques, coupled with increased imports of cotton textiles from India, created new and interesting fabrics specifically for use in curtaining.

"More elaborate" and "theatrical" are the most common descriptions of all window coverings of the Baroque Era. Cornices and pelmets gained importance as the preferred method of finishing the top of a window treatment, their primary function being to conceal the rods and workings of the curtains mounted beneath. Cornices were made of wood and usually hand carved in

very intricate patterns. A pelmet differs from a cornice in that it is usually made of stiffened fabric, shaped and often embellished with hand-made, decorative edgings.

Passementerie, the art of making decorative trims, flourished during the reign of Louis XIV in France. Later the Huguenots, facing religious persecution, fled to Germany, England and the Netherlands taking with them the skills of their intricate crafts.

The beautiful trimmings initially used to disguise the seams and joins on draperies evolved into decorative details reserved for royalty and nobility. Flat braids, tasseled fringes and soutache made of fine silk yarns adorned the edges of velvets, brocades and damasks during the height of the Baroque era.

DREAM WINDOWS

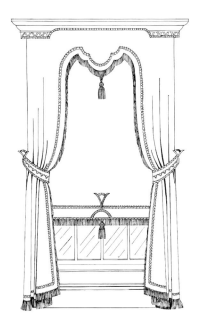

Window curtains had previously been simple, single panels of fabric. The innovation of designing them in pairs created symmetry on the window. These sets of curtains were usually tied back with a piece of fabric or a metal holdback during the day and drawn across the window for privacy at night.

Daniel Marot, a French artist and upholsterer of the seventeenth century, is credited with designing the "festoon", a drapery that can be pulled up on the window creating a swagged effect. From this concept, many varied styles of blinds and valances developed, of which the swag and tail style valance are most notable.

Sashes provided sun control on windows during the day. These were made of very fine, sheer fabric, stretched onto a frame and soaked in oil. The frame was mounted against the window and the oil soaked fabric became translucent, providing a sun barrier.

Bed canopies also became more elaborate during the Baroque era. The actual wood structure was smaller than during the Renaissance, but the bed hangings and curtains reached new levels of opulence and detailing. Rich embroidered tapestries and silks often were draped from rods mounted under the wood structure.

Early Georgian was the decorative style of England and America during the Baroque period in Europe. While the Early Georgian look was greatly influenced by the French Baroque, it was implemented in a more refined and simplified way. Many of the designs that define Early Georgian are attributed to Sir Christopher Wren, the Royal Architect of England during the late 1600's.

The most significant concept that developed during the Late Georgian period was the idea of matching window curtains and bed hangings. Previously, these two elements were regarded as unrelated in the interior design of a room. Rich damasks and brocades in gold, blue and red hues were now used for both draperies and bed enclosures. Other colors that dominated interior design during this era included turquoise, teal and coral.

Bed hangings were commonplace throughout Europe by this time, providing warmth and decoration to the stately rooms of the era. Cotton chintz fabrics, block print-ed in English garden patterns, were more affordable for the middle class of this time, and increased the popular-ity of these furnishings. Households of the wealthy would have two sets of bed hangings, a heavy tapestry fabric for winter months and lighter muslin fabric for summer.

Elegantly shaped and elaborately embellished pelmets dominated the silhouette of the Late Georgian period. Appliqué and embroidery techniques further enriched the look of the designs. Billowing fes-toon blinds, which were pulled up under the pelmets by means of cords, were regarded as the most fashionable look in Europe.

Window treatments during the Late Georgian Era could be described as more fluid. The newest fabrics and designs had a soft flow not previously achieved in window coverings. Adding to this feeling of movement was the use of ribbons and garlands as motifs on patterned fabrics.

"Italian stringing", or reefed curtains, were more popular during this time in England. These drapery panels were made to create a festooned look by pulling a string diagonally toward the upper outside corners of the window causing the curtain fabric to billow and swag gracefully. Interior designers today still use this very elegant method of creating a festoon.

The oil soaked sashes of the Baroque era were still in common use as a means of sun control during this time. Often hand painted with intricate designs or outdoor scenes, the sashes became the precursor to roller shades, which were introduced toward the end of this period.

Roller blinds were made of natural linen or cotton and used a pulley system to be raised or lowered for sun control and privacy.

Window coverings were becoming more complex as architects began designing window styles and shapes based on the proportions established by sixteenth century Italian architect Andrea Palladio's ideals, called the Palladian principles. These were a specific set of proportions based on the classical architecture of ancient Greece that could be applied to various exterior elements, including windows.

Upholsterers from the Baroque through the Victorian Eras were solely responsible for the interior design of a home. The finely-made bed hangings and window treatments were the designs of these skilled and influential men. They dutifully commissioned and supervised the various trades required to execute their lavish designs. One such man was Thomas Chippendale.

In 1754, Chippendale published a pattern book of designs, "The Gentleman and Cabinet-Makers Director". This book remained a great influence in the interior design trade for many years. Chippendale commonly used motifs of Chinese influence as well as the trademark shell design of the Rococo period. These motifs were used in fabric patterns, as well as the richly-carved wooden structure of beds and other furniture.

Window shapes of this era posed many difficulties, as they often do today. The Gothic-peaked window and Palladian-arch window were common throughout Europe and Britain. Chippendale created curved pelmet boards and lambrequins to decorate these windows and then draped them with softly folded swags. Much of this era took on a lighter approach to draperies

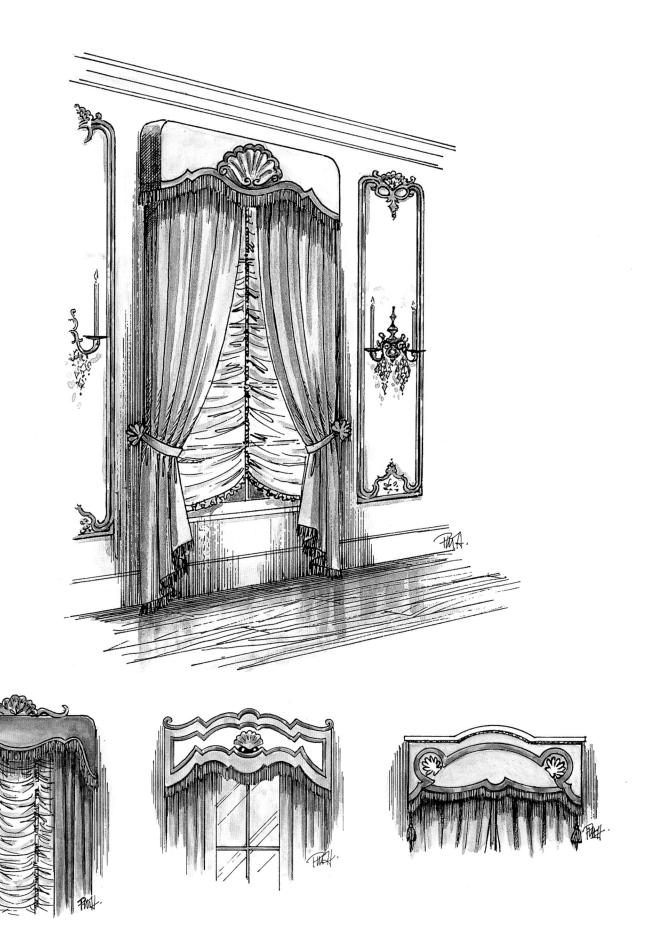

ROCOCO/LOUIS XV 23

DREAM WINDOWS

Pull-up curtains, and what were referred to as "Roman drapery curtains", were the most fashionable window coverings of the day. Additional fullness was included in the styling of the pull curtains, giving them a softer look. These curtains were paired with draperies of a richer, darker fabric on top or with an embellished pelmet.

Developments in the textile industry during this era allowed for the creation of fabrics that would take on timeless qualities. "Toiles de Jouy" was a printed fabric from the village of Jouy in France. It literally means the work of Jouy and is the origin of fabric that today is known simply as toile. Toile was the first fabric to be printed using the copperplate method. This method produced fabrics that had better definition of design and allowed for a larger repeat. Glazing fabrics to produce "chintz" was also introduced during this time.

The wooden structure of the bed was redefined in several variations as canopies adopted a lighter look. The "half tester" was a shorter canopy that projected out from the wall over a portion of the bed rather than the whole length. "Lit a la polonaise" was a domed canopy supported by rods on each of the four corners and disguised by beautiful silk panels. In France, it had become common to place beds in alcoves and build lambrequins graced with side panels around them.

and bed hangings, favoring a greater desire for comfort. Lightweight silk taffeta called "quinze-seize" was the most common fabric for window curtaining and was made in the new lighter hues that typified this period. Colors were more refined; soft pastels in yellow, pink and blue replaced the dark jewel tones of the previous century.

Cotton and silk replaced heavier fabrics such as velvet and tapestry used for the canopies and bed hangings during the Baroque era. The Rococo period marked the transition from the very ornate and elaborate style in the Baroque Era to a refined and classic style that dominated the neoclassic period of the late eighteenth century.

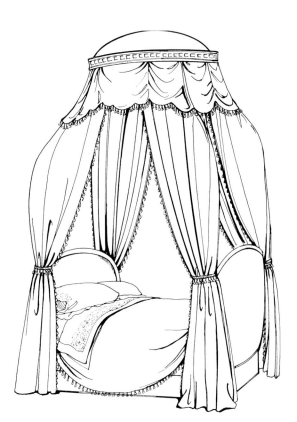

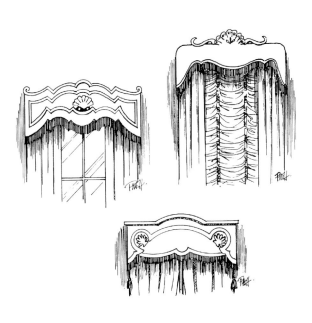

Neoclassic 1770 - 1820

Neoclassicism is an elegant style of design characterized by simple, geometric forms. Ancient Greek and Roman Classical artifacts, found in the excavations at Pompeii and Herculaneum during the 1700's, inspired this styling.

NEOCLASSIC

The designing of beds and bed canopies became the responsibility of the cabinetmaker rather than the upholsterer at this time. This resulted in less focus on the bed hangings as well as the introduction of coordinated cornices for both the bed and window. One cabinetmaker whose designs were influential in the late 1700's was Thomas Sheraton.

Sheraton was renowned for unique beds and elaborate cornices. The introduction of the "Pagoda" cornice, with a distinctly Chinese influence, is credited to Sheraton. His designs, published in the 1793 pattern book "Cabinet-maker and Upholsterer's Drawing Book", were carved and gilded with Classical motifs.

Draperies, made in pairs for symmetry, were the most common style of window covering in the Neoclassic Era. This simpler look led to the need to improve the rods used for decorative purposes or functionality. The introduction at this time of the first cord and pulley style rod, now known as a traverse rod, reduced wear and tear on draperies.

Discoveries at these ruins also inspired popular colors during the Neoclassic Era. A palette of earth tones including clay, terracotta and green were all accented with black. Other influences for decorative colors came from industry rather than history. Wedgwood pottery inspired a range of blue colors that was popular at this time, and the colors used in the tapestry factories Aubusson and Gobelins in France also contributed to the color trends of the time.

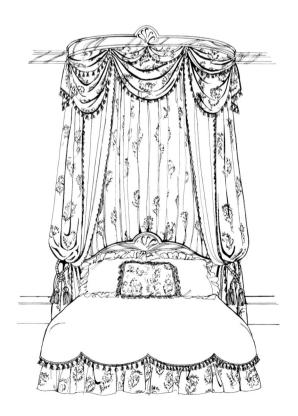

NEOCLASSIC

DREAM WINDOWS

These new rods had an overlap in the center that greatly enhanced the finished look of the draperies. In addition, decorative rods with elaborate finials and rings gave interest and balance to the simplicity of the silhouette of this time.

Layers of curtains were added beneath the over drapes as sheers gained popularity. These muslin curtains were installed onto the window frame to provide added privacy and sun protection in a room.

The biggest technological achievement in the production of decorative textiles in this era was the invention of the Jacquard loom by Joseph Jacquard in 1804. This complex loom allowed the most intricate patterns to be woven into fabric by machine, something that could only be done painstakingly, by hand, in the past.

Toward the end of the Neoclassic period, the sharp symmetry that silhouetted the drapery styling was replaced by an asymmetrical look that was later popularized in the Empire period.

Once health concerns arose that bed hangings and canopies reduced air circulation and attracted dust and that wooden structures housed insects, open beds made of iron replaced them. This resulted in a greater emphasis on bed coverings and window treatments during the Empire and Regency Periods.

With the same concerns that saw the demise of the canopy bed, pelmets and cornices also began to play less importance. Window treatments maintained a look of opulence as multiple layers of curtains were now used,

often in an asymmetrical styling. It was not uncommon for a window to have 4 or 5 individual layers of curtains - an over drape, an under curtain made of a lighter-weight fabric, a sub curtain and blinds, and possibly a swag valance mounted over the entire ensemble.

The popularity of the sheer sub curtain continued to rise during the Empire period. Made of silk or cotton muslin, these became standard window coverings in neutral hues. Alternatively, glass curtains, also made of muslin, were used in less formal room settings and fitted

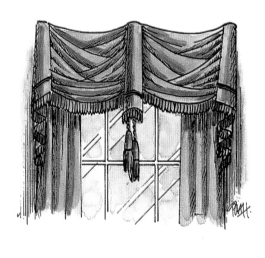

on the lower half of the window, next to the panes of glass. History suggests that both types of curtain served to protect against unwanted insects entering through open windows and to filter the light from the sun.

The elimination of pelmets and cornices necessitated in refining and designing more intricate drapery headings and rods. French pleats, goblet pleats and smocked headings maintained folds in a more regulated and decorative manner while rods became opulent display pieces. Made of brass or wood, the finials and brackets of these rods took inspiration from classic motifs such as laurel and acanthus leafs, and military ornamentation such as spearheads and eagles.

"Continued drapery", a term used to describe the practice of disguising two or more separate windows as one by means of a continuous valance or rod, easily lent itself

to the asymmetrical designs of this era. Each window alone was asymmetrical, but when coupled with the other windows within the arrangement, the mirror image would create a balanced effect.

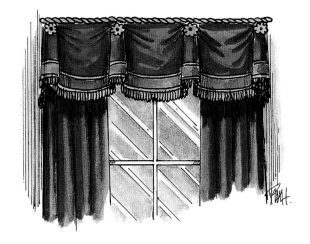

The popularity of the puddled drapery increased during the Empire period. Designers of the time differed in opinion as to what length was appropriate, from a few inches hanging gracefully on the floor to yards of fabric creating a more dramatic, puddled effect.

Historians also differ in opinion as to the reason for the extra length of fabrics used in what some termed "receptacles for dust". Some believe that the length of draperies represented wealth: the more fabric that a

Historically, window treatments evolve in cycles of lavishness and opulence to periods of understated simplicity with transitory periods building up to a crescendo. The layered styling of the Empire and Regency periods was the transitory time cresting toward the opulent look of the Victorian Era.

person could afford, the wealthier that they were. Others believe that it was purely functional: to stop drafts from the window. This is especially likely since the bed hangings of previous times had been eliminated.

Another decorative detail widely used throughout this time was reverse lining. A secondary fabric could give the effect of an additional layer of drapery, when used as the lining of the main drapery, which was turned back or reversed to reveal the contrast fabric.

Roller blinds added an artistic element to interior design. These became the canvases for landscape paintings and printed designs. Sometimes trimmed with fringe or borders, roller blinds were often an integral part of a window treatment during this period.

The Victorian Era was a complex period with many different phases defining it. Historians agree, however that it was a time of excessiveness and clutter. The multiple layers of curtaining that dominated the silhouette were a reflection of the extravagant look of the Victorian interior. As in the past, it was not unusual for a window treatment to consist of four or five layers of curtains.

Details using fabrics and fringes were the trend. Bands of contrast fabric were often applied to the edges of draperies and valances. The much heavier look of Bouillon fringe replaced tassel fringe and braids.

Lace grew in popularity for use as under curtains and glass curtains. Machine made laces and netting made these fabrics more affordable to the middle class. Lace or sheer panels were gathered onto brass rods and either

DREAM WINDOWS

smaller and less ornate than those of earlier periods, though still gilded and sometimes augmented with brass ornamentation.

Lambrequins, the elongated version of the cornice, which extends down the sides of a window, had been in vogue during the Empire and early Victorian eras but became obsolete by the end of the nineteenth century. It was felt that these large structures were too heavy for the interiors of the day and that they blocked out too much light.

hung freely at the bottom or attached to the window frame with a second rod at the hem. When used in bedrooms or on doors, these panels would be tied with ribbon, pulling in at the center and creating an hourglass effect.

Respected designers of the time advised their clients on the importance of adding lining and interlining to draperies. Not only would the lining extend the life of the fabric, it would provide thermal qualities and help prevent other furnishings from becoming bleached by the sun.

It was the opinion of noted designer John Loudon that draperies could not perform the function of preventing drafts unless a cornice valance was used. This wooden box would close off the space at the top of the curtains that could allow cold air to circulate. The cornices used during this era were

New designs in fabric window shades were evolving. More fabric and fullness were constantly being added to create soft billows. The Austrian shade, with smaller, closely-sewn festoons, was the result of this. Swag and tail valances were often paired with the Austrian curtain for a refined, elegant look.

Roller shades, now manufactured with spring mechanisms, remained an important window covering for privacy and sun control. Other blinds that became highly developed during this time were the wooden horizontal blind and louvered shutters.

Critics of the excessiveness of the Victorian Era started a reform group advocating more simplicity in styling and a return to Gothic design principles. This came to be known as the Aesthetic Movement. William Morris, a name synonymous with decorative fabrics, was a founder of the Aesthetic Movement in interior design. He and other influential designers, such as Charles Eastlake, objected to the suffocating, overly-draped look of the high Victorian Era. Their designs were kept simple and functional so as to serve only as a background to the room's interior.

The ideals of the Aesthetic Movement prevailed until the end of the nineteenth century when a revival movement reintroduced the French-influenced styling of draperies, returning once again to elaborate cornices, over drapes, under drapes and all the embellishments that typify the window treatments of eras gone by.

Opposite
Soft, sheer swags & panels grace an elegant window

Right
The simple Roman shade is a beautiful compliment to the luxurious silk draperies

Bottom
Goblet pleat drapes with button detailing

Lower bottom
An asymmetrical style using small knife pleats

While Europeans find the terms curtains and draperies to be interchangeable, Americans find the pair anything but synonymous. Utilizing heavier, lined fabrics, draperies offer a more formal choice than curtains which make use of lighter, sheer materials. Yet no matter what the desired effect, draperies can take shape as an uncomplicated, sill- length window treatment or a floor-length work of art. Whether in a soft-white bedroom or a period-style dining room, draperies offer a wonderful opportunity to maintain the genre of any space as they effortlessly harmonize with furniture pieces and wall décor. Draperies can also act as a prelude as textures and colors hint to what lay on the other side of the window - a vibrantly green oak tree, a richly red rose bush or a delicately blue ocean. With an almost overwhelming variety of choices, draperies can fulfill the simplest of needs to the most demanding of tastes. Though sometimes

Opposite Top
Tri-colored sheers gathered onto crane rods

Opposite Bottom
View of windows with open crane rods

Top
Goblet pleat silk drapes with sheer under curtains

Bottom
Pleated drapes with contrast banding, mounted on wooden poles

Top
Gothic inspired valance with side panels and Roman blinds

Bottom
Contrast braid creates tab top drapes. Coordinating Roman valance

Opposite top right
Asymmetrical side panel with contrast band mounted on iron rod

Opposite bottom
Room view of asymmetrical panels complement the décor

a more expensive choice, draperies possess many advantages that accompany their aesthetic value. Whether a window is large or small, draperies offer a comforting sense of privacy from the world outside the home. Warmth can also be found in draperies as they can help to protect from a cool winter's night. While nestled in your favorite chair - whether to read a few chapters of a good book or to take a relaxing, afternoon nap - draperies will always accommodate the most specific of lighting needs. And regardless of taste and desire for formality, in a chameleon-like nature, draperies will both complement and enhance the existing style of any room in your home.

Top left opposite
Pleated drapes with contrast bands and buttons. Simple valances on side windows to compliment the look

Top right opposite
Detail of smocked heading

Mid right opposite
Detail of contrast buttons on pleats

Bottom opposite
Elegant silk velvet drapes with smocked heading

Top
Contemporary swags create this very elegant treatment trimmed with tassels and rosettes

Bottom left
These attractive leaded windows are complemented with an upholstered box valance, tunnel top drapes and contour tiebacks

Bottom right
Sheer tunnel top drapes on brass rods with streamer tiebacks add a charming touch to an entryway

Pinch (French) Pleated Draperies

PINCH PLEATED SPECIFICATIONS

DESCRIPTION:

A window covering topped with decorative pinched folds. Although a simple treatment on its own, it creates a complete look when used under valances or over sheers. Can be a functional or decorative treatment when used with tiebacks.

YARDAGE:

Step 1

Width of area to be covered x 2.5 ÷ width of fabric = number of widths (whole numbers only)

Step 2a

Number of widths x (length of window + 16") ÷ 36 = yardage without pattern repeat

or

Step 2b

Length + 16" ÷ pattern repeat = number of repeats required (round upward to nearest whole number)

Step 2c

Number of repeats required x pattern repeat = cut length

Step 2d

Number of widths x cut length ÷ 36 = yardage with pattern repeat

WORK ORDER SPECIFICATIONS:

1. Width
2. Length
3. Color of lining
4. Center split, no center split or panel
5. Specify type of rod being used
6. Is treatment going over other treatments?
7. Tiebacks required - see section on tiebacks

SPECIAL NOTE:

A check measure is recommended for all full length drapes.

Shirred (Smocked) and Pencil Heading Draperies

SHIRRED SPECIFICATIONS

DESCRIPTION:
An attractive heading that creates even gathers across the width of the drapes. It adds a soft, romantic look to a simple window treatment.

YARDAGE
Step 1
Width of window x 2.5 ÷ width of fabric = number of widths (whole numbers only)

Step 2a
Number of widths x (length of area to be covered + 16") ÷ 36 = yardage without pattern repeat
or

Step 2b
Length + 16" ÷ pattern repeat = number of repeats required (round upward to nearest whole number)

Step 2c
Number of repeats required x pattern repeat = cut length

Step 2d
Number of widths x cut length ÷ 36 = yardage with pattern repeat

WORK ORDER SPECIFICATIONS:
1. Width
2. Length
3. Color of lining
4. Tiebacks required
5. Center split, off center split, or panel

SPECIAL NOTE:
1. A check measure is recommended for all full length drapes.
2. Shirred drapes should stay stationary due to the nature of the heading.

Box-Pleated Draperies

BOX-PLEATED
SPECIFICATIONS

DESCRIPTION:

An interesting alternative to the traditional pinch pleat, box pleats create the very tailored styling of this drape. For optimum effect and function, use either as a stationary treatment with tiebacks or with a decorative rod.

YARDAGE:

Step 1
Width of area to be covered x 3 ÷ width of fabric = number of widths (whole numbers only)

Step 2a
Number of widths x (length + 16") ÷ 36 = yardage without pattern repeat

or

Step 2b
Length + 16" ÷ pattern repeat = number of repeats required (round upward to nearest whole number)

Step 2c
Number of repeats required x pattern repeat = cut length

Step 2d
Number of widths x cut length ÷ 36 = yardage with pattern repeat

WORK ORDER SPECIFICATIONS:

1. Width
2. Length
3. Color of lining
4. Center split, off center split or panel
5. Specify type of rod being used
6. Is treatment going over other treatments?
7. Tiebacks required

SPECIAL NOTE:

1. A check measure is recommended for all full length drapes.
2. Reduce fullness to 2 ½ if using a traverse rod.

Tab Draperies

DREAM WINDOWS

TAB DRAPERY SPECIFICATIONS

DESCRIPTION:
The simple styling of this treatment enhances the beauty of a decorative rod. Fabric loops (tabs) sewn to the top of a flat panel give this treatment a very contemporary look.

YARDAGE:
Step 1
Width of area to be covered x 1.5 ÷ width of fabric = number of widths (whole numbers only)

Step 2a
Number of widths x (length of area + 24") ÷ 36 = yardage without pattern repeat
or

Step 2b
Length + 24" ÷ pattern repeat = number of repeats required (round upward to nearest whole number)

Step 2c
Number of repeats required x pattern repeat = cut length

Step 2d
Number of widths x cut length ÷ 36 = yardage with pattern repeat

WORK ORDER SPECIFICATIONS:
1. Width
2. Length
3. Color of lining
4. Diameter of rod being used

SPECIAL NOTE:
1. Yardage calculations include tabs.
2. Only one and a half times fullness is required on this treatment to obtain the proper effect.

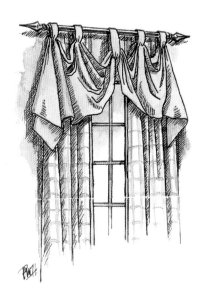

ATHENA DRAPERY SPECIFICATIONS

DESCRIPTION:
This elegant style is created from a flat panel. Rings or brass clips are attached sufficiently apart so as to create a softly swagged effect at the heading when on the rod. The drape gracefully falls on the floor, puddle style. A facing of self or contrast fabric is required so that the lining will not show at the heading.

YARDAGE:
Step 1
Width of area to be covered x 2 ÷ width of fabric = number of widths (whole numbers only)
Step 2a
Number of widths x (length + 16") ÷ 36 = yardage without pattern repeat
or
Step 2b
Length + 16" ÷ pattern repeat = number of repeats required (round upward to nearest whole number)
Step 2c
Number of repeats required x pattern repeat = cut length
Step 2d
Number of widths x cut length ÷ 36 = yardage with pattern repeat
For self or contrast facing: Allow ¼ yd. per width

WORK ORDER SPECIFICATIONS:
1. Width of area to be covered
2. Length
3. Color of lining
4. Specify fabric for facing
5. Center split or panel
6. Type of rod, rings being used

SPECIAL NOTE:
1. A puddle of 6" has been allowed in yardage. If more is desired, add to length + allowance.
2. Soft, drapeable fabrics create the best effect.

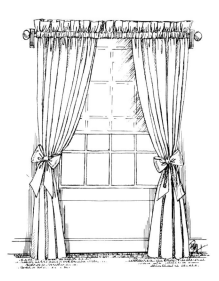

ROD POCKET
SPECIFICATIONS

DESCRIPTION:

A drapery treatment that creates a shirred heading look by gathering fabric onto a rod. The treatment can be dressed with a ruffle above the rod, or without, if being used under a valance. Rod pocket covers can also be used to separate panels.

YARDAGE:

Step 1

Width of area to be covered x 2.5 divided by width of fabric = number of widths (whole numbers only)

Step 2a

Number of widths x (length of area + 16") divided by 36 = yardage without pattern repeat

or

Step 2b

Length + 16" divided by pattern repeat = number of repeats required (round upward to nearest whole number)

Step 2c

Number of repeats required x pattern repeat = cut length

Step 2d

Number of widths x cut length divided by 36 = yardage with pattern repeat

WORK ORDER SPECIFICATIONS:

1. Width
2. Length
3. Color of lining
4. Size of rod being used
5. Center split or panel
6. Tiebacks required
7. Inside or outside mount
8. Frill size on top of rod (if applicable)

SPECIAL NOTE:

l. This is a stationary treatment.
2. This treatment cannot be used when treatment underneath is mounted up to the ceiling.
3. Extra yardage has to be calculated for rod covers.

Tuxedo (Pull-Back) Draperies

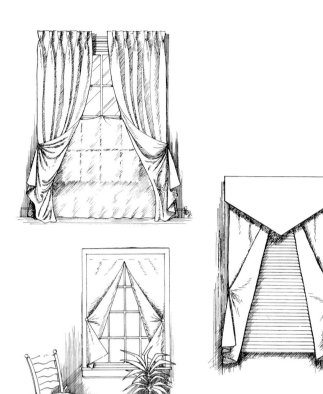

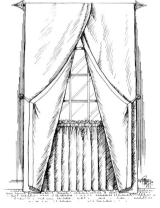

TUXEDO (PULL-BACK)
SPECIFICATIONS

DESCRIPTION:
A contemporary version of a traditional look that consists of a flat or pleated panel simply folded back and tied to reveal the contrast lining.

YARDAGE (For Flat Panels Only):
Step 1
Width of area being covered + return + 5" divided by width of fabric = number of widths (whole numbers only)
Step 2a
Number of widths x (length of area + 10") divided by 36 = yardage without pattern repeat
Or
Step 2b
Length + 10" divided by pattern repeat = number of repeats required (round upward to nearest whole number)
Step 2c
Number of repeats required x pattern repeat = cut length
Step 2d
Number of widths x cut length divided by 36 = yardage with pattern repeat
Step 3
Calculate with same formula for contrast lining
Step 4
Allow ½ yard for ties, 1 yard for larger sash ties

WORK ORDER SPECIFICATIONS:
1. Width
2. Length
3. Inside or outside mount
4. Size of returns needed
5. Specify which fabric is to be used as contrast

SPECIAL NOTE:
1. Large returns are not recommended for this treatment.
2. Tuxedo drapes limit the amount of light into a room.
3. Not recommended for windows that are proportionately wider than longer.

FLAT ROD POCKET DRAPERY
SPECIFICATIONS

DESCRIPTION:

A drapery treatment where a 2 ½" or 4 ½" shirred heading look is created by gathering fabric onto a flat rod. Two flat rods can be used to create a deeper heading look.

YARDAGE:

Step 1

Width of area to be covered + 10" x 2.5 ÷ width of fabric = number of widths (whole numbers only)

Step 2a

Number of widths x (length + 20") ÷ 36 = yardage without pattern repeat

or

Step 2b

Length + 20" ÷ pattern repeat = number of repeats required (round upward to nearest whole number)

Step 2c

Number of repeats required x pattern repeat = cut length

Step 2d

Number of widths x pattern repeat ÷ 36 = yardage with pattern repeats

WORK ORDER SPECIFICATIONS:

1. Width
2. Length
3. Color of lining
4. Size of rod needed or being used
5. Center split or no center split
6. Tiebacks required
7. Number of tunnels

SPECIAL NOTE:

This is a stationary treatment which will require tiebacks or a rod cover to separate panels.

ROD TOP AND BOTTOM SPECIFICATIONS

DESCRIPTION:
A drape where the fabric is stretched between two rods creating an all-over shirred effect. An excellent treatment if privacy is required or if working with a narrower window. Add a collar tieback to create a decorative hourglass shape.

YARDAGE:
Step 1
Width of area to be covered x 2.5 divided by width of fabric = number of widths
Step 2a
Number of widths x (length of area + 16") divided by 36 = yardage without pattern repeat
or
Step 2b
Length + 16" divided by pattern repeat = number of repeats required (round upward to nearest whole number)
Step 2c
Number of repeats required x pattern repeat = cut length
Step 2d
Number of widths x cut length divided by 36 = yardage with pattern repeat

WORK ORDER SPECIFICATIONS:
1. Width
2. Length
3. Color of lining
4. Size of rods being used
5. Inside or outside mounts
6. Frill size top and bottom of rod

SPECIAL NOTE:
l. Stationary treatment.
2. Not recommended for windows larger than 48".
3. A frill is recommended for this treatment to conceal hardware.

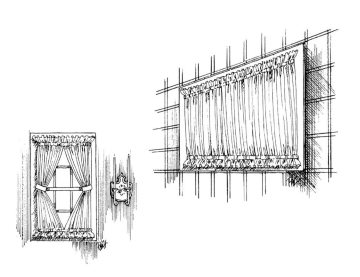

TIEBACKS

DESCRIPTION:

A decorative accent by which drapes and curtains are tied back. The various styles give a personal touch to the window treatment.

YARDAGE:

Standard
  1/2 yd.
Standard with Piping
  1/2 yd. + 1/2 yd. Piping
Standard with Banding
  1/2 yd. + 1/2 yd. Banding
Standard with Bows
  1/2 yd. + 1 yd. Bows
Contour
  3/4 yd.
Ruched Tieback
  1 yd.
Ruffled Tieback
  1/2 yd. + 1 1/2 yd. Ruffle
Streamer Tieback
  2 yds.
Braided Tieback
  1/2 yd.
  each strand (3 strands)
Collar with Hook and Loop
Fastener
  1/2 yd.

WORK ORDER SPECIFICATIONS:

1. Style
2. Fabric if contrasts are used

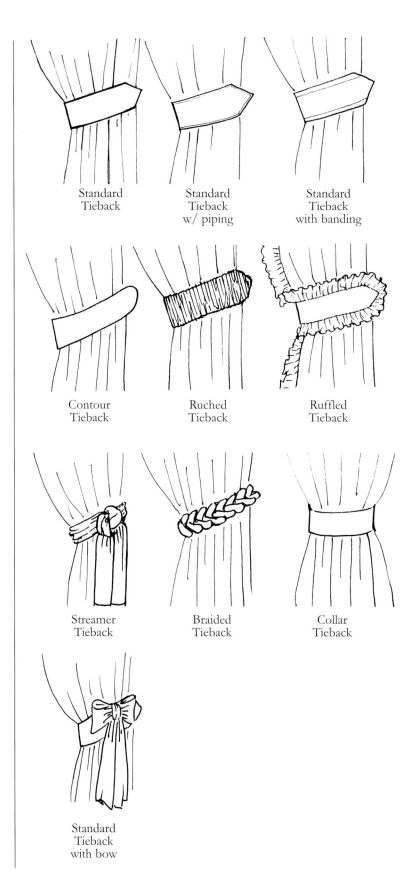

Standard
Tieback

Standard
Tieback
w/ piping

Standard
Tieback
with banding

Contour
Tieback

Ruched
Tieback

Ruffled
Tieback

Streamer
Tieback

Braided
Tieback

Collar
Tieback

Standard
Tieback
with bow

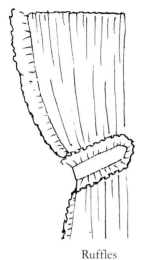

Ruffles

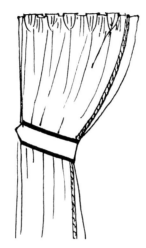

Inset
Banding

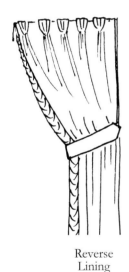

Reverse
Lining

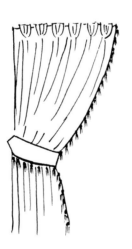

Fringe

Personal Touches

DESCRIPTION:

There are many details that may be added to personalize a window treatment. Ruffles add charm and romance to the look of a room. Use on drapes, tiebacks, cushions or comforters for a country look.

Insert banding adds dramatic contrast to a window treatment. A band of 2" or more is sewn inset from the edges.

Reverse lining is a decorative facing sewn to the lining, then folded outwards to reveal the contrast and held in place with tiebacks.

Fringe and braids used decoratively on a window treatment echo the elegance of past eras.

YARDAGE:

Ruffles:
    1/4 yd. for each 24" Ruffles
Inset Banding:
    Length + hem allowances
Reverse Lining:
    Length + hem allowances
Fringe and Brais:
    Length + additional 10%

**WORK ORDER
SPECIFICATIONS:**

Clearly indicate treatment and fabrics.

Sunburst

DESCRIPTION:

Decorative accent for an arched window. The sunburst is softly gathered into the center and usually in a sheer or lace fabric to enhance the window and filter the light. A rosette may be added.

YARDAGE:

For 118" sheer or lace -- 1 1/2 yds.
For 48" lace -- 3 1/2 yds.
Windows up to 48" in diameter

WORK ORDER SPECIFICATIONS:

1. Specify fabric
2. Specify if a rosette is desired
3. A template of window should be provided

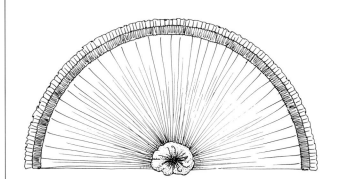

Dressing Tables and Stools

DESCRIPTION:

A romantic detail to add to the most feminine bedroom. The separate cover is gathered in two styles, balloon or ruffled. Upholstered stools coordinate with either style.

YARDAGE:

Ballon style:
Top and balloon skirt - 7 yds.
Underskirt - 5 yds.
Bows - 2 yds.
Ruffled style:
Skirt - 10 yds.
Contrast bow - 1/2 yd.
Stool:
Skirt - 3 1/2 yds.
Bows - 1/2 yd. (for 2)

WORK ORDER SPECIFICATIONS:

1. Style of table
2. Fabric details

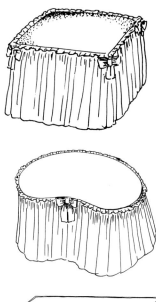

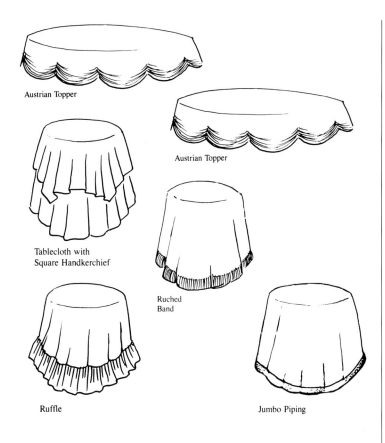

Austrian Topper

Austrian Topper

Tablecloth with
Square Handkerchief

Ruched
Band

Ruffle

Jumbo Piping

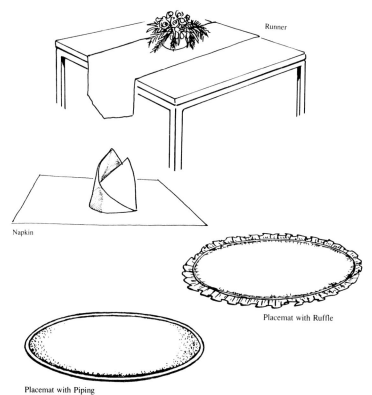

Runner

Napkin

Placemat with Ruffle

Placemat with Piping

TABLECLOTHS AND TOPPERS

DESCRIPTION:

Decorative tablecloths and toppers can complement any room decor. The tablecloth is finished with piping at the bottom and may have jumbo piping, ruched band or ruffles added. Table toppers complete the look in a basic square handkerchief, stylish Austrian or box pleated.

YARDAGE:

	up to 74" diameter	up to 90" diameter
Round Tablecloth with		
Regular Piping	4 3/4 yds.	6 yds.
For Jumbo Piping	add 1 1/2 yds.	add 1 1/2 yds.
For Ruched Band	add 2 1/2 yds.	add 3 yds.
For Ruffle	add 4 yds.	add 5 yds.
Square Handkerchief		
Topper (50")	1 1/2 yds.	1 1/2 yds.
Austrian Topper	2 3/4 yds.	3 1/2 yds.
Pleated Topper	2 3/4 yds.	3 1/2 yds.

WORK ORDER SPECIFICATIONS:

1. Diameter of table
2. Drop measurement to floor
3. Style of tablecloth or topper
4. Fabric details

NAPKINS PLACEMATS AND RUNNERS

DESCRIPTION:

Quilted placemats custom made to your color scheme. Finished with piping or a 1" ruffle. Coordinating 18" square dinner napkins are double hemmed and stitched. Runners add a decorative touch that display a fine wood or glass table to its best advantage.

YARDAGE:

Placemats

Print fabrics - 18-27" pattern repeat; allow 1 repeat per placemat
Plain or small prints - allow 1/2 yd. per placemat
For Ruffle add - 1/4 yd. per placemat

Napkins

Print fabrics - 18" - 27" pattern repeat 1 1/2 yds. = 4
Plain or small print - 1 1/4 yds. = 4

Runners

Length of table + 24" ÷ 36 = number of yards

WORK ORDER SPECIFICATIONS:

l. Fabric details
2. Sizes

UPHOLSTERED MIRRORS

DESCRIPTION:

The ultimate in custom decor – fully upholstered mirrors. Fabric may be ruched onto frame or pulled flat and finished around the edges with matching piping or ruffles.

YARDAGE:

Ruched – 2 yds.
Flat – 1 1/4 yds.
Piping – add 1/2 yd.
Ruffle – add 1 1/4 yds.

WORK ORDER SPECIFICATIONS:

1. Style of mirror
2. Size of mirror
3. Fabric details

COVERED RODS

DESCRIPTION:

For a truly customized window treatment, fabric covered wooden rods and finials add decorating flare. A swag casually draped over a rod or drapes on cafe rings are two excellent ways in which this treatment can be used.

YARDAGE:

For Rod and Finial:
Up to 60" wide – allow 1 yd.
Up to 108" wide – allow 1 1/2 yds.
Up to 144" wide – allow 2 yds.

WORK ORDER SPECIFICATIONS:

1. Size and diamenter of rod
2. Fabric details

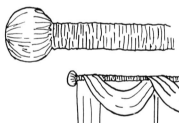

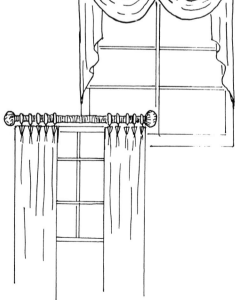

SHOWER CURTAINS

DESCRIPTION:

From practical to stylish to extravagant, the shower curtain can often be the focal point of a bathroom. First introduced in 1810 along with a crude form of the modern shower, it serves both utilitarian and aesthetic purposes. Swags, installed at the ceiling level, give added opulence. Ornamental tie-backs also add elegance. For a more decorative look, replacing ordinary curtain rings with ribbons, grommets or decorative rings can add a hint of flair.

YARDAGE:

54" fabric, 27" repeat, 11 yds.
48" fabric, no repeat, 13 yds.

YARDAGE:

Standard shower curtain
72" x 72" requires:
Solid fabric or small print -
5 yds.
Large print - 5 1/2 yds.

WORK ORDER SPECIFICATIONS:

Fabric details

SPECIAL NOTE:

Mock curtains using shirred or pleated heading and tiebacks may also be used by installing into ceiling.

Fabric Shades

Left
An interesting contrast is created when red bands were applied to this balloon shade

Above
This cloud shade made in a calico print is perfect for this log cabin retreat

From Victorian to Art Deco to modern, fabric shades are a fitting contribution to almost every decorating style. Their simplicity allows them to accompany other window treatments while their classic lines allow them to stand on their own. For an especially appropriate choice, a fabric shade can be a splendid addition to odd shaped windows, such bay, round or tall, or those found on stairwells. In a child's room, a fabric shade can empty the space beneath the window, and in kitchens, their lack of interlining will keep odors from lingering in the fabric.

To determine between the many types of fabric shades, one must only consider the methods in which these window treatments are raised. Austrian blinds, also known as festoons, are gathered, both horizontally and vertically, for a full look. Sewn to the back are rows of rings,

Top
Shirred roman shades made of silk add to the grace of
this window

Opposite Top
The luxury of this bathroom is enriched with a balloon
shade of silk and tassels
Opposite Bottom
A roman valance is given interest with contrast "straps"

through which is threaded the pulley system. Though the rows can be drawn simultaneously, the inner rows can be lifted independently for an arched look. So that the fabric may balloon, a lighter fabric is perfect for an Austrian shade. When let down, they have the swagged effect of a curtain, and when pulled up they give the appearance of a valance.

Roman shades present a more modern silhouette. With their bold lines and clean, tailored edges, this type of shade makes an attractive solitary window treatment. Due to its rows of rings, unlike the Austrian shade, the Roman shade is drawn up in crisp, horizontal folds. It may be embellished with a trim at the base of each tuck or castellated edge. Its simplicity is also complimentary to a more dramatic drapery or valance. Strong fabric choices for Roman shades include sheer cottons, linens and corded silks. Large, bold patterns may look strange with the shade folded up, so it is better to choose a solid, textured fabric or a smaller pattern such as gingham, stripes or checks.

Also known as Holland blinds, roller shades are economical, practical and simple to use. In the early nineteenth century, they were often painted with pastoral scenes or elaborate designs. Although these types of embellishments are now uncommon, there are other ways to add a touch of extravagance, such as pairing the shades with sophisticated window treatments or adding decorative edges. Roller shades are usually made from closely woven burlap, Holland cotton or canvas, and can be made with a chain-operated pulley as an alternative to the common spring mechanism.

Top
Roman shades are perfect in this neutral decor
Bottom
Detail photo of Roman shade

Opposite Top Left
A wooden cornice was painted to coordinate the silk damask used in this balloon shade
Opposite Top Right
Stripes are the perfect fabric for a Roman shade
Opposite Bottom
The simple, tailored look of Roman shades are ideal in this family room

Top Left
Flouncy and fun describes this balloon with tassel & cord trim

Top Right
Contrast banding gives this Roman shade a dramatic effect

Bottom
A balloon shade frames this unusually shaped window

Opposite Right
Balloon shades are an elegant treatment for this fully coordinated room

DREAM WINDOWS

DREAM WINDOWS

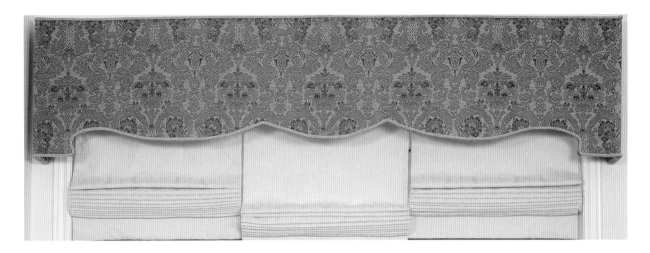

Top
A Scalloped cornice softens the tailored look of the Roman shades

Bottom left
Silk Balloons trimmed with bouillon fringe

Mid-Right
Roman blinds are the perfect compliment in this wood paneled library

Bottom Right
Roman shade with decorative trim

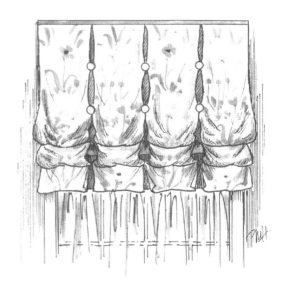

DREAM WINDOWS

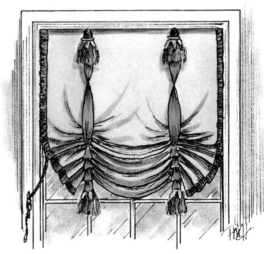

FABRIC SHADES

DREAM WINDOWS

FABRIC SHADES

FABRIC SHADES

Cloud Shades

DESCRIPTION:
Fully functional shade with a gathered heading that falls into soft poufs which can be finished with or without a skirt.

YARDAGE:
Step 1
Width of window + returns x 2.5 ÷ width of fabric = number of widths (whole numbers only)
Step 2a
Number of widths x (length of shade + 20") ÷ 36 = yardage without pattern repeat
or
Step 2b
Length of shade + 20" ÷ pattern repeat = number of repeats required (round upward to nearest whole number)
Step 2c
Number of repeats required x pattern repeat = cut length
Step 2d
Number of widths x cut length ÷ 36 = yardage with pattern repeat

WORK ORDER SPECIFICATIONS:
1. Width
2. Length
3. Color of lining
4. Inside or outside mount
5. Skirt or no skirt
6. Size of returns or size of board
7. Ceiling or wall mount
8. Right or left pull

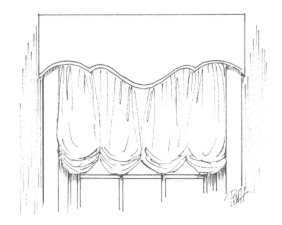

BALLOON SHADES

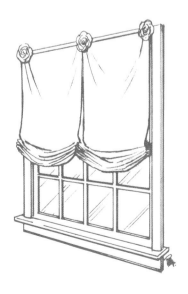

DESCRIPTION:
Fully functional shade with large inverted pleats for a more tailored look that is softened by billowing poufs.

YARDAGE:
Step 1
Width of window + returns x 3 ÷ width of fabric = number of widths (whole numbers only)
Step 2a
Number of widths x (length of shade + 20") ÷ 36 = yardage without pattern repeat
or
Step 2b
Length of shade + 20" ÷ pattern repeat = number of repeats required (round upward to nearest whole number)
Step 2c
Number of repeats required x pattern repeat = cut length
Step 2d
Number of widths x cut length ÷ 36 = yardage with pattern repeat

WORK ORDER SPECIFICATIONS:
1. Width
2. Length
3. Color of lining
4. Inside or outside mount
5. Size of returns or size of board
6. Ceiling or wall mount
7. Right or left pull

FLAT ROMAN SHADES

DESCRIPTION:

A versatile shade that hangs straight and falls into folds as it is raised. The Roman shade fits many different décors from contemporary to traditional to formal. To add interest to the blind, use contrast bands, a scalloped edge or a single permanent pleat at the bottom.

YARDAGE:

Step 1

Width of area to be covered x 5" ÷ width of fabric = number of widths (whole numbers only)

Step 2a

Number of widths x (length of area + 12") ÷ 36 = yardage without pattern repeat

or

Step 2b

Length of window + 12" ÷ pattern repeat = number of repeats required (round upward to nearest whole number)

Step 2c

Number of repeats required x pattern repeat = cut length

Step 2d

Number of widths x cut length ÷ 36 = yardage with pattern repeat

WORK ORDER SPECIFICATIONS:

1. Width
2. Length
3. Color of lining
4. Inside or outside mount
5. Right or left pull

SPECIAL NOTE:

1. Roman shades are not recommended wider or longer than 84".
2. Cannot be made with returns.

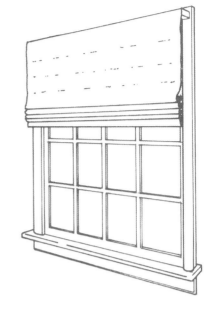

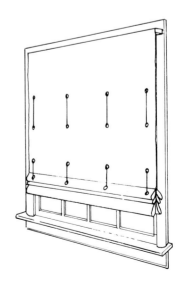

FOLDED ROMAN SHADES

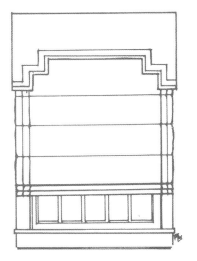

DESCRIPTION:
A folded Roman is designed with overlapping folds cascading down the full length of the shade.

YARDAGE:
Step 1
Width of window + 5" ÷ width of fabric = number of widths (whole numbers only)
Step 2a
Number of widths x (length of window x 2.5) ÷ 36 = yardage without pattern repeat
or
Step 2b
Length of window x 2.5 ÷ pattern repeat = number of repeats required (round upward to nearest whole number)
Step 2c
Number of repeats required x pattern repeat = cut length
Step 2d
Number of widths x cut length ÷ 36 = yardage with pattern repeat

WORK ORDER SPECIFICATIONS:
1. Width
2. Length
3. Color of lining
4. Inside or outside mount
5. Left or right pull

SPECIAL NOTE:
1. Folded Romans larger than 60" in width or 84" in length are not recommended.
2. Due to the nature of fabric, the folds do not hang evenly, therefore they are not recommended for an application where two or more blinds are side by side.
3. Returns are not applicable to Romans.

Shirred Roman Shades

DESCRIPTION:
Soft gathers add romance to the look of a traditional Roman shade. Fabric is shirred onto rods to create this very elegant yet functional shade.

YARDAGE:

Step 1
Width of window x 3 divided by width of fabric = number of widths (whole numbers only)

Step 2a
Length of window x 1.25 x number of widths ÷ 36 = yardage without pattern repeat

or

Step 2b
Length of window x 1.25 ÷ pattern repeat = number of repeats required (round upward to nearest whole number)

Step 2c
Number of repeats required x pattern repeat = cut length

Step 2d
Number of widths x cut length ÷ 36 = yardage with pattern repeat

WORK ORDER SPECIFICATIONS:
1. Width
2. Length
3. Cord - right or left
4. Inside or outside mount
5. Lining color (if applicable)

SPECIAL NOTE:
1. Use only soft drapeable fabrics for optimum effect.
2. This treatment cannot be made with returns and therefore is intended to be used alone or as an undertreatment.
3. Not recommended wider than 60".

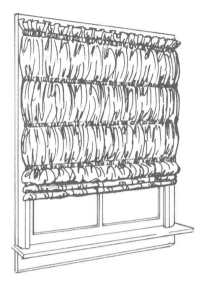

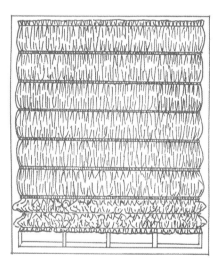

AUSTRIAN SHADES

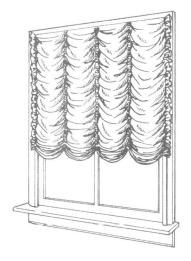

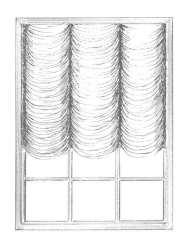

DESCRIPTION:

A soft formal treatment created by vertical shirring between scallops. Use heavier fabric for privacy. Sheer or lace fabric for a more decorative look. It can be used as a single treatment or in combination with over drapes and valances.

YARDAGE:

Step 1
(Width of area to be covered x 1.5) ÷ width of fabric = number of widths (whole numbers only)

Step 2a
Number of widths x (length of area x 3) ÷ 36 = yardage without pattern repeat

or

Step 2b
Length of area x 3 ÷ pattern repeat = number of repeats required (round upward to nearest whole number)

Step 2c
Number of repeats required x pattern repeat = cut length

Step 2d
Number of widths x cut length ÷ 36 = yardage with pattern repeat

WORK ORDER SPECIFICATIONS:

1. Width
2. Length
3. Color of lining (if applicable)
4. Inside or outside mount
5. Right or left cord pull

SPECIAL NOTE:

This treatment has a tendency to pull in on the sides. It should not be used where this will cause a problem.

Valances and Cornice Boxes

Left
A tear drop swag leaves an unobstructed view of this beautiful yard

Top
Double layers of jabots cascade over an upholstered box

Whether standing alone or as an accompaniment to an existing window treatment, valances and cornice boxes can be an exquisite addition to any home. While essential to a period room, a pelmet can also find its place among a modern, country design or an intricate bay window. Yet the possibilities with valances and cornice boxes are endless.

Why not create a tabbed valance woven with tulips and daisies in a shade of yellow found in the kitchen table chairs? What about pairing an elaborately colored Kingston valance with rich, burgundy draperies in a classically-formal living room? How about softening a set of

DREAM WINDOWS

Left
The softly shaped edge of this cornice compliments the feminine look of this bath

Top
A Savannah valance is gathered over a balloon shade and drapery panels

wooden, vertical blinds with a pale, violet cloud valance to add a touch of color to a home office?

Though a permanent window treatment, a cornice box is anything but sedentary. Situated atop a tall window, an intricately carved cornice box can transport the room to a time when kings and queens lived amongst overwhelming opulence. And a shaped cornice above a child's window - adorned with tigers, lions and giraffes -

Top
A Roman valance with tabs gives a contemporary look when mounted with an iron rod

Left
An upholstered box and pleated drapery over wooden blinds

Right
A cloud valance adds to the celestial theme of this nursery

Left
An upholstered box valance with sheer curtains gives balance to this room's interior

Top
A pelmet valance with soft pleats is mounted over tuxedo style side panels

can contribute to a theme whose potential is as far reaching as the child's imagination.

With the unlimited potential of valances and cornice boxes, anything is possible when adding these window treatments to your home.

DREAM WINDOWS

Left
The beautiful symmetry of this room is created with upholstered cornices and side panels of silk damask

Top
A richly patterned chenille valance is mounted over double layers of drapery panels

Opposite Top
Velvet adds to the richness of this upholstered cornice and side panels

Opposite Bottom Left
Detail of double layer of side panels

Opposite Bottom Right
Chinese influenced shaping detail

Bottom
Layers of silk create this beautiful treatment. Windsor swags, balloons and side panels

DREAM WINDOWS

Opposite Top
Multiple rows of fabric covered piping give a 3D effect
to these cornices
Opposite Bottom
Gathered valances on flat rods and side panels
Top
A tailored look-upholstered box valance and side panels

CLOUD VALANCE

DESCRIPTION:

This window treatment is used to suggest a cloud shade yet it cannot be raised or lowered. Used for its softening effect on the window, the gathered heading falls into soft poufs that can be finished with or without a skirt. A cloud valance can be used alone if privacy is not a factor, or as a decorative finish over other window treatments, such as vertical blinds, drapes or Venetian blinds.

YARDAGE:

Step 1
Width of window + returns x 2.5 ÷ width of fabric = number of widths (whole numbers only)

Step 2a
Number of widths x (length of valance + 16") ÷ 36 = yardage without pattern repeat

or

Step 2b
Length of area + 16" ÷ pattern repeat = number of repeats required (round upward to nearest whole number)

Step 2c
Number of repeats required x pattern repeat = cut length

Step 2d
Number of widths x cut length divided by 36 = yardage with pattern repeat

WORK ORDER SPECIFICATIONS:
1. Width
2. Length
3. Color of lining
4. Inside or outside mount
5. Skirt or no skirt
6. Size of returns or size of board
7. Ceiling or wall mount

SPECIAL NOTE:

For valances shorter than 16", a functional cloud that can be raised to the correct height is recommended. See Cloud Shade.

BALLOON VALANCE

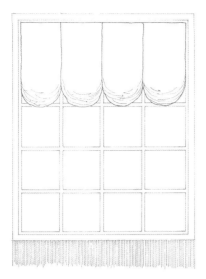

DESCRIPTION:
A window treatment to suggest a balloon shade yet it cannot be raised or lowered. Large inverted pleats create a more tailored effect that is softened by billowing poufs. It can be used alone if privacy is not a factor, or as a decorative finish over other window treatments, such as vertical blinds, drapes or Venetian blinds.

YARDAGE:
Step 1
Width of window + returns x 3 ÷ width of fabric = number of widths (whole numbers only)
Step 2a
Number of widths x (length of valance + 16") ÷ 36 = yardage without pattern repeat
or
Step 2b
Length of valance + 16" ÷ pattern repeat = number of repeats required (round upward to nearest whole number)
Step 2c
Number of repeats required x pattern repeat = cut length
Step 2d
Number of widths x cut length ÷ 36 = yardage with pattern repeat

WORK ORDER SPECIFICATIONS:
1. Width
2. Length
3. Color of lining
4. Inside or outside mount
5. Size of returns or size of board
6. Ceiling or wall mount

SPECIAL NOTE:
For valances shorter than 16", a functional balloon that can be raised to the correct height is recommended. See Balloon Shade.

POUF VALANCE AND FESTOON VALANCE

POUF DESCRIPTION:
A soft billowing valance, similar to a cloud, but the effect is one continuous pouf rather than separate poufs and it will not have skirt.

YARDAGE:
Step 1
Width of area to be covered + returns x 2.5 ÷ width of fabric = number of widths
Step 2a
Length + 10" x number of widths ÷ 36 = yardage without pattern repeat
or
Step 2b
Length + 10" divided by pattern repeat = number of repeats required (round upward to nearest whole number)
Step 2c
Number of repeats required x pattern repeat = cut length
Step 2d
Number of widths x cut length divided by 36 = yardage with pattern repeat

WORK ORDER SPECIFICATIONS:
1. Width
2. Length
3. Returns if applicable
4. Color of lining

FESTOON DESCRIPTION:
The same romantic softness of a cloud but constructed with a separate ruffle that flounces the sides and around the scallops. It can be used over Venetian blinds, pleated shades, etc.

YARDAGE:
Step 1
Width of area to be covered + returns x 2.5 divided by width of fabric = number of widths
Step 2a
Length + 12" x number of widths ÷ 36 = yardage without pattern repeat
or
Step 2b
Length + 12" divided by pattern repeat = number of repeats required (round upward to nearest whole number)

Step 2c
Number of repeats required x pattern repeat = cut length
Step 2d
Number of widths x cut length ÷ 36 = yardage with pattern repeat

WORK ORDER SPECIFICATIONS:
1. Width
2. Length
3. Returns
4. Size of ruffle
5. Fabric details
6. Color of lining

Savannah Valance and Legacy Valance

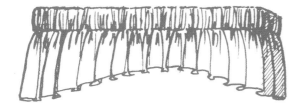

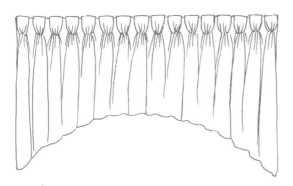

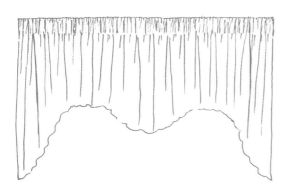

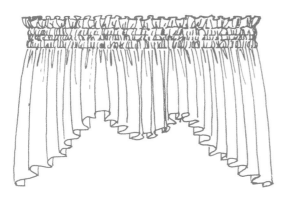

DESCRIPTION:
Softly shaped valances add an interesting touch to a window without distorting the view. A legacy valance differs from the Savannah valance with a dip in the center. Heading may be pleated, shirred or tunneled.

YARDAGE:
Step 1
Width of area to be covered + returns x 2.5 divided by width of fabric = number of widths required

Step 2a
Length to longest point + 16" x number of widths divided by 36 = yardage without pattern repeat
or

Step 2b
Length to longest point + 16" divided by pattern repeat = number of repeats required (round upward to nearest whole number)

Step 2c
Number of repeats required x pattern repeat = cut length

Step 2d
Number of widths x cut length divided by 36 = yardage with pattern repeat

WORK ORDER SPECIFICATIONS:
1. Width
2. Returns
3. Length to longest point
4. Length to shortest point
5. Length to mid-point (for legacy valance)
6. Fabric details
7. Type of heading

SPECIAL NOTE:
A check measure and installation are strongly recommended. If using a shirred heading, a wood and hook and loop fastener mount is recommended.

ROMAN VALANCE

DESCRIPTION:

This window treatment is used to suggest a Roman shade yet it cannot be raised or lowered. A variety of decorative trims or contrast bands may be used to add interest. It is finished with two permanent pleats.

YARDAGE:

Step 1

Width of area to be covered + 4" ÷ width of fabric = number of widths required

Step 2a

Length + 16" x number of widths ÷ 36 = yardage without pattern repeat

or

Step 2b

Length + 16" ÷ pattern repeat = number of repeats required (round upward to nearest whole number)

Step 2c

Number of repeats required x pattern repeat = cut length

Step 2d

Number of widths x cut length divided by 36 = yardage with pattern repeat

WORK ORDER SPECIFICATIONS:

1. Width
2. Length
3. Inside or outside mount
4. Color of lining
5. Details of banding (if applicable)

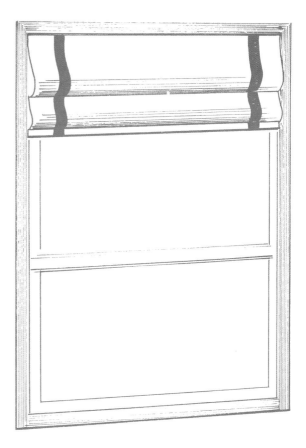

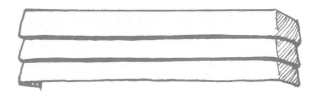

AUSTRIAN VALANCE

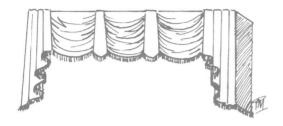

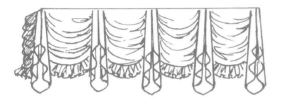

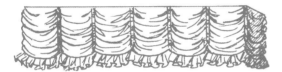

DESCRIPTION:
A soft formal valance created by vertical shirring between scallops. Combine with other treatments to create a complete look.

YARDAGE:
Step 1
Width of area to be covered + returns x 1.5 ÷ width of fabric = number of widths (whole numbers only)

Step 2a
Number of widths x (length of valance x 3) ÷ 36 = yardage without pattern repeat

or

Step 2b
Length of valance x 3 ÷ pattern repeat = number of repeats required (round upward to nearest whole number)

Step 2c
Number of repeats required x pattern repeat = cut length

Step 2d
Number of widths x cut length divided by 36 = yardage with pattern repeat

WORK ORDER SPECIFICATIONS:
1. Width
2. Length
3. Color of lining
4. Inside or outside mount
5. Returns

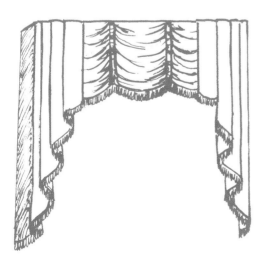

Upolstered Valance Boxes

DESCRIPTION:
Upholstered valances provide a classic topping for windows of any size, making an excellent overtreatment for drapes, vertical blinds or Venetian blinds. The valance is constructed of a wooden frame that is padded and upholstered in a decorative fabric and finished with piping on the top and bottom edges.

YARDAGE: See Box Below

WORK ORDER SPECIFICATIONS:
1. Width
2. Length - shortest + longest points
3. Return
4. Style
5. Fabric details
6. Color of lining

SPECIAL NOTE:
1. A check measure and installation is strongly recommended.
2. Off center prints may create an unbalanced effect, so choose fabric carefully.

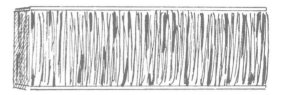

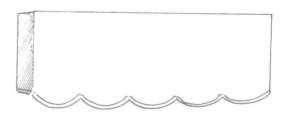

Style	Width		
	48" to 84"	84" to 120"	120" to 144"
Tailored	2 yds.	3 yds.	3½ yds.
Square Notch	2 yds.	3 yds.	3½ yds.
Scallop	2 yds.	3 yds.	3½ yds.
Scroll	2 yds.	3 yds.	3½ yds.
Ruched	3 yds.	4½ yds.	5½ yds.

BOX-PLEATED VALANCE

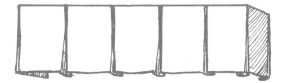

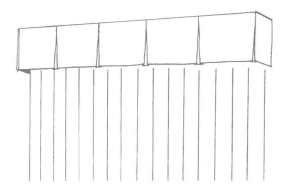

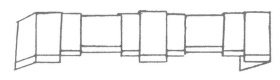

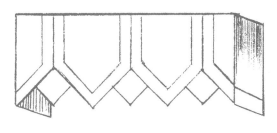

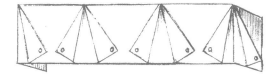

DESCRIPTION:
A very tailored style that lends itself well as an overtreatment with vertical blinds, Venetian blinds and tied back drapes. Contrast banding adds a crisp look.

YARDAGE:
Step 1
Width of area to be covered + returns x 3 ÷ width of fabric = number of widths required
Step 2a
Length of valance + 6" x number of widths ÷ 36 = yardage without pattern repeat
or
Step 2b
Length of valance + 6" ÷ pattern repeat = number of repeats required (round upward to nearest whole number)
Step 2c
Number of repeats required x pattern repeat = cut length
Step 2d
Number of widths x cut length ÷ 36 = yardage with pattern repeat

WORK ORDER SPECIFICATIONS:
1. Width
2. Length
3. Returns
4. Color of lining
5. Contrast banding if applicable

SPECIAL NOTE:
1. A check measure and installation are strongly recommended.
2. Pleats are sized to window and pattern usually 10" to 12".

Top
Swags, cascades and jabots in perfect balance

Right
A contrast band and piping are used to create
interest in this simple style

Swags and Cascades

As diverse as they are versatile, swags and cascades can assume many roles in the world of home decor. They may take the lead as they dominate the stage you have set for your audience to enjoy. They may step into a supporting role alongside an elegant set of draperies or a modest vertical blind. Or they may simply be an extra – standing quietly in the background, fulfilling their part. In their most subtle form, a swag and cascade combination can take shape as a sheer, off-white fabric that entwines itself around an unassuming pole or rod. With the hardware moderately exposed, the designer is pre-sented with a tempting opportunity to explore their imagination. And you may choose to encourage that exploration with finials embellished with mouth-water-ing pineapples, foreboding spears or humble gargoyles. For a more involved role in the home, a swag and cas-cade may find themselves in the company of simple draperies swept to the side with tie-backs, allowing the sun's warmth to discover the room. Or perhaps the com-bination will take their place framing a pair of refined French doors which open upon an elaborate, backyard garden. When wanting to steal the spotlight, the task is

Top
An asymmetrical, free flowing swag with tassels and cording
Bottom
A contemporary swag on pole and bishop sleeve panels
Right
An elongated swag with fabric poufs and matching panels tied back

Right
Decorative hardware
creates a focal point
for the softly draped
swags

Bottom
Arched swags with
layers of cascades
and side panels in an
elegant dining room

an easy one for swags and cascades. A bay window can become a stage set for royalty when rich, green fabric becomes a blending of deep swags, floor length cascades, golden, tasseled rope and precisely placed rosettes. And no matter how large or small the role may be, a swag and cascade combination is sure to make a statement.

Top
Pole swags in a traditional overlapping formation with long side panels

Opposite Top
Silk draperies are highlighted with a beautiful swag valance
Opposite Bottom Left
The elaborately carved rod is exposed above the swag
Opposite Bottom Right
Multi layered swags and cascades make a rich and beautiful treatment

Top
Decorative holdbacks are used to position the swags of this very tall window

Left
Fringe, cording and tassels give this swag valance extra detail

DREAM WINDOWS

SWAGS AND CASCADES

DREAM WINDOWS

DESCRIPTION:

Overlapping swags draped gracefully across the width of the window make an elegant and formal window treatment. Jabots, the decorative side pieces, are constructed to create a cascading effect.

YARDAGE:

Swags:

1 1/2 yards each

Jabots:

Finished length of jabot + 10" x 2 ÷ 36 = yardage with pattern repeat

or

Finished length of jabot + 10" + pattern repeat x 2 ÷ 36 = yardage with pattern repeat; allow same yardage for contrast or self-lining in jabots

WORK ORDER SPECIFICATIONS:

1. Swag formation: Traditional, Regency or Georgian style
2. Color of lining in swags
3. Contrast or self-lining jabots
4. Width, length of swags, length of jabots
5. Number of swags
6. Returns

SPECIAL NOTE:

1. Each swag is constructed approximately 30" wide. When overlapped, the area a swag covers is approximately 20".
2. A check measure and installation are strongly recommended.
3. Not recommended for bay windows, see Linear Swags.

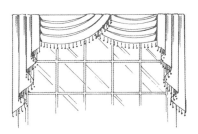

Contemporary Swags and Jabots

DESCRIPTION:

Swags are draped beautifully across the window and can be used with a decorat-ice rod and constructed to appear as if the fabric is casually thrown over the rod, or constructed as one large swag that is mounted on wood.

YARDAGE:

For one swag:
Width of the window + 30% ÷ 36 = yardage
More than one Swag:
Width of the window + 50% ÷ 36 = yardage
Jabots:
Length of jabots + 10" x 2 ÷ 36 = yardage without pattern repeat
or
Length of jabots + 10" + pattern repeat x 2 ÷ 36 = yardage with pattern repeat; allow same yardage for contrast or self-lining in jabots and swags

WORK ORDER SPECIFICA-TIONS:

1. Color of lining in swags
2. Lining of jabots - self lined or con-trast
3. Width, length of swags and jabots
4. Number of swags
5. Wood and hook and loop fastener mount or decorative rod

SPECIAL NOTE:

1. These swags are cut on a straight grain of fabric. Any fabric with an obvious directional print is not suitable.
2. Proportions are very important with this type of swag.
3. Check measure and installation are strongly recommended.
4. Not applicable for bay windows.

DESCRIPTION:

A graceful variation of the ever popular swag valance. Soft, unstructured swags gather into conical pleats. A complete look on its own or jabots may be added for extra decoration. Self- or contrast-lining is required.

YARDAGE:

Swag valance:
1 1/2 yards each
Jabots (if applicable):
Finished length of jabot + 10" x 2 ÷ 36 = yardage without pattern repeat
or
Finished length of jabot + 10" + pattern repeat x 2 ÷ 36 = yardage with pattern repeat
Lining for Swags and Jabots:
Allow same yardage

WORK ORDER SPECIFICATIONS:

1. Width of area to be covered
2. Length of swags (short point, long point)
3. Length of jabots (if applicable)
4. Returns
5. Specify lining

SPECIAL NOTE:

To archieve proper proportions, consult with workroom.

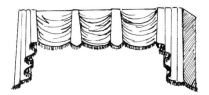

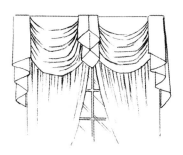

LINEAR SWAGS AND JABOTS

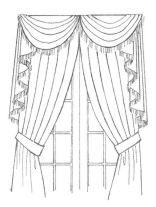

DESCRIPTION:

Most commonly used in a bay window where overlapping swags are inappropriate. Swags are butted together and sewn end to end. Decorative cascades and/or rosettes are used to conceal the seams of the swags and the heading of under-drapes. Jabots are still used as the finishing touches on each end.

YARDAGE:

Swags:
18" to 30" wide - 1 1/2 yards each
Cascades:
1 1/2 yd. each
Jabots:
Length of jabot + 10" x 2 ÷ 36 = yardage without pattern repeat
or
Length of jabot + 10" + pattern repeat x 2 ÷ 36 = yardage with pattern repeat; allow same yardage of contrast or self-lining in jabots.

WORK ORDER SPECIFICATIONS:

1. Color of lining in swags
2. Contrast or self-lining jabots
3. Width, length of swags, jabots and cascades
4. Number of swags
5. Returns

SPECIAL NOTE:

To ensure correct proportions, consult with workroom.

Alternative Window Treatments

If a set of goblet-pleated draperies seems too costly or an Egyptian-print swag and cascade combination seems too dramatic, there are many alternatives to these fabric-based window coverings. Yet when searching for a straightforward approach to window treatments, practical need not be unimaginative. There are many charismatic options for those who prefer a lighter touch.

There are simple, vinyl roller shades for the kitchen windows and woven-wood shades that will happily compliment a living room filled with deep-green furnishings, an abundance of plants and Hibiscus flowers and a Tiki statue looking on from the corner. There are stained wood Venetian blinds for the window above your desk and modest vertical blinds

which fit nicely across wide-sliding doors. There are panel shutters that can take a bay window back to the days of Scarlett O'Hara and there are louvered shutters that can be opened just enough so the family cat can spy on the nest of unsuspecting sparrows. And no matter what alternative window covering you decide upon, it is certain that your shades, blinds or shutters will fulfill your needs for visual impact and light control while they provide you with a calming sense of privacy.

For some, the bedroom is merely a place to sleep. For others, it is a playroom, a reading room or a quiet place to catch up on some work. Yet no matter how much time one spends in the bedroom, the look and feel of the space is of utmost importance. And thankfully, it is space with boundless options which extend well beyond the decision between draperies and shutters. When beginning to design in the bedroom, there are an infinite number of starting points. Whether choosing the windows, the flooring or the walls, eventually you will come to the bedding. A well-chosen bedspread can quietly blend with a complex color scheme or can easily become the focal point of the room. Surrounded by an exotic swag and cascade combination or sophisticated floral

Opposite
A smocked canopy adds architectural interest to this bed treatment.

Top
Tunnel-top draperies with banded tiebacks are the perfect complement to a multi-colored bed treatment

Right
A matching cloud valance contributes to the cozy warmth of a window seat

draperies, a light, blue bedspread, that compliments one of the many colors in the room, may be just enough. For a more augmented involvement, a pink and gray gingham bedspread may find its place in a room with a perfectly-matched valance, surrounded by simple walls and pale pink pillows. And when a bedspread is ready to become the centerpiece of a bedroom, the fabric can become as vivacious as reality will allow, as window treatments, armoires and carpeting fall into place to complement the ingenuity.

Top
This fairytale bedroom is created with festoon valances, pinch pleated drapes and shirred valances, ruffled toss cushions and decorative accents to the comforter

Top
Cloud shades give this bathroom a soft touch, while tunnel top and bottom sheers ensure privacy

Right
A pretty comforter is given added interest with a scalloped hem; the bedskirt and tablecloth finish off the look

BEDROOMS AND BATHROOMS

BED CANOPIES

DESCRIPTION:

The crowning detail of a lavish bed treatment. Valances are mounted onto a semicircular piece of wood. Self- or contrast-lined panels drape gracefully to the floor and are held in place with streamer tiebacks.

YARDAGE:

See chart on the right

WORK ORDER SPECIFICATIONS:

1. Size of bed, length to floor
2. Style of canopy
3. Specify fabrics and details

	TWIN	DOUBLE/ QUEEN	KING
Shaped Savanah Valance (includes self-lining)	5 yds.	6 yds.	7 yds.
Side Panels	8 yds.	12 yds.	12 yds.
Self- or contrast-lining	8 yds.	12 yds.	12 yds.
Streamer tiebacks	1 yd.	1 yd.	1 yd.
Festoon Valances (includes self-lining)	5 yds.	6 yds.	7 yds.
Ruffle for Valance	2 1/2 yds.	2 3/4 yds.	3 1/4 yds.
Side Panels	8 yds.	12 yds.	12 yds.
Self-or contrast-lining	8 yds.	12 yds.	12 yds.
Ruffle for side panels	3 yds.	3 yds.	3 yds.
Streamer tiebacks	1 yd.	1 yd.	1 yd.

1. The yardage allowances are based on the following:

    54" Wide fabric / 37" repeat
    96" Length -- ceiling to floor
    12" Allowance for pouf
    1 Width each panel for twin bed
    1 1/2 Widths each panel for Double, Queen, King

ANY VARIATIONS FROM THIS WILL AFFECT THE YARDAGE

2. Approximate dimensions of wood are:

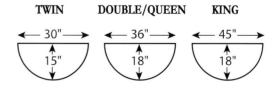

TWIN   DOUBLE/QUEEN   KING

30"   36"   45"
15"   18"   18"

THROW BEDSPREADS

DESCRIPTION:

An Outline or channel quilted bedcovering which falls loosely over the bed. It can be made with a full drop or, if there is a footboard, a half drop can be used in conjunction with a bedskirt. Usually completed with a pillow tuck or reverse sham.

Details such as scallops and ruffles can be added to create different, more elaborate designs.

YARDAGE:

	Pillow Tuck	Reverse Sham
Twin / Full Drop	9 yds.	9 yds.
Double / Full Drop	9 yds.	9 yds.
Queen / Full Drop	13 yds.	13 1/2 yds.
King / Full Drop	13 1/2 yds.	13 1/2 yds.
Twin / Half Drop	7 1/2 yds.	7 1/2 yds.
Double / Half Drop	7 1/2 yds.	9 yds.
Queen / Half Drop	9 yds.	9 yds.
King / Half Drop	11 1/2 yds.	13 1/2 yds.

WORK ORDER SPECIFICATIONS:

1. Color of lining
2. Bed measurements, width and length
3. Specify drop measurement from top of mattress to floor for full drop or specify desired measure
4. Specify pillow tuck or reverse sham

SPECIAL NOTE:

1. Throw bedspreads cannot have split corners
2. See Personal Touches: Bedspreads for extra details
3. Pattern is quilted at workroom's discretion

DUVET COVERS AND PERSONAL TOUCHES: BEDSPREADS

DESCRIPTION:

A large "pillow case" that protects your duvet and creates a decorative look. Finish with piping or use some flare by adding ruffles, jumbo piping or ruched piping.

YARDAGE:

See Chart Below

WORK ORDER SPECIFICATIONS:

1. Size of duvet
2. Note all details and fabrics

Ruched Piping

Ruffle

Ruffle with Piping

Jumbo Piping

Double Ruffle

PERSONAL TOUCHES: BEDSPREADS

DESCRIPTION:

Add your own personal flare to a bedspread. Ruffles, scallops and jumbo piping create a custom finish.

YARDAGE:

Comforters/Bedspreads
Ruffles	add 5 yds.
Jumbo Piping	add 2 yds.
Ruched Piping	add 5 1/4 yds.
Scalloped Edge with Piping	add 2 yds.

Bedspreads with Reverse Sham
Ruffles	add 7 yds.
Jumbo Piping	add 3 yds.
Ruched Piping	add 7 yds.
Scalloped Edge with Piping	add 3 yds.

WORK ORDER SPECIFICATIONS:

Specify details and fabric

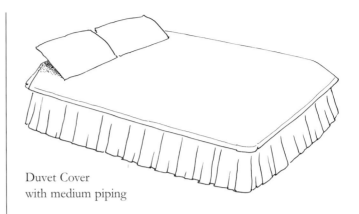
Duvet Cover
with medium piping

Duvet Covers One Side Only	54" Fabric 27" Repeat	48"Fabric No Repeat
Twin	6 yds.	5 1/4 yds.
Double	6 yds.	5 1/4 yds.
Queen	6 yds.	5 1/2 yds.
King	6 yds.	8 yds.
Details		
Medium Piping	add 1 1/4 yds.	
Jumbo Piping	add 1 3/4 yds.	
Ruched Piping	add 3 1/4 yds.	
3" Ruffle	add 3 1/4 yds.	
4" Ruffle	add 4 1/4 yds.	

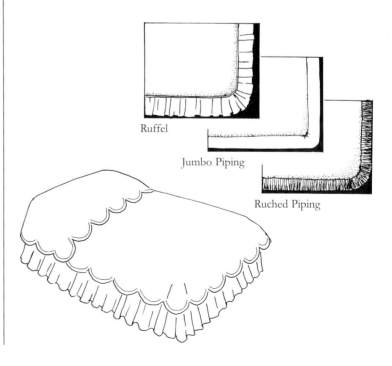
Ruffel

Jumbo Piping

Ruched Piping

Gathered Drop Bedspread And Comforters

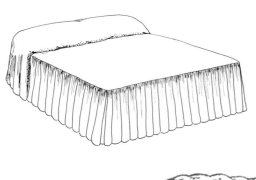

DESCRIPTION:

Bedspread is outline or channel quilted on top, piped along the edge and softly gathered along sides, dropping gracefully to the floor. This style lends itself well to a four-poster bed.

YARDAGE:

Twin	6 yds.
Double	6 yds.
Queen	7 1/2 yds.
King	9 yds.

WORK ORDER SPECIFICATIONS:

1. Width and length of mattress
2. Drop to floor
3. Should corners be split?
4. Color of lining
5. Pillow tuck or reverse sham

COMFORTERS

DESCRIPTION:

An outline or channel quilted throw covering with only a 12" drop. Used in conjunction with pillow shams and bedskirts. Details such as scallops, ruffles or pipin can be added for that personal touch.

YARDAGE:

Twin	6 yds.
Double	6 yds.
Queen	7 1/2 yds.
King	9 yds.

WORK ORDER SPECIFICATIONS:

1. Color of lining
2. Bed measurement: width, length

SPECIAL NOTE:

1. Drop is always 12", if longer see Bedspreads
2. See Personal Touches: Bedspreads for extra details, yardages
3. Pattern is quilted at workroom's discretion

BEDSKIRTS

DESCRIPTION:

A bedding treatment to dress the box spring. It's the finishing touch used with comforters, half drop bedspreads and duvet covers. Bedskirts come in styles such as gathered, tailored, box pleated and cluster gathered.

YARDAGE:

See chart on the right

WORK ORDER SPECIFICATIONS:

1. Color of lining
2. Box measurement width and length
3. Drop measurement from top of box spring to floor
4. Specify style of bedskirt

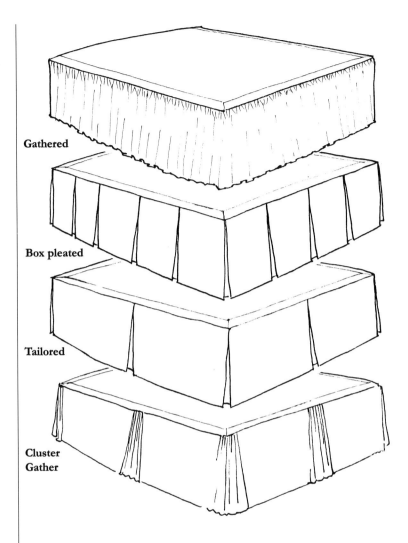

Gathered

Box pleated

Tailored

Cluster Gather

	54" Fabric 27" Repeat	48" Fabric No Repeat
Tailored/Cluster Gathered		
Twin	4 1/2 yds.	3/4 yds.
Double	6 yds.	4 3/4 yds.
Queen	6 yds.	5 yds.
King	7 1/2 yds.	6 yds.
Gathered/Box Pleated		
Twin	6 3/4 yds.	5 1/4 yds.
Double	7 1/2 yds.	5 3/4 yds.
Queen	8 1/4 yds.	6 1/2 yds.
King	9 yds.	7 yds.

DAYBED COVER AND BOLSTERS

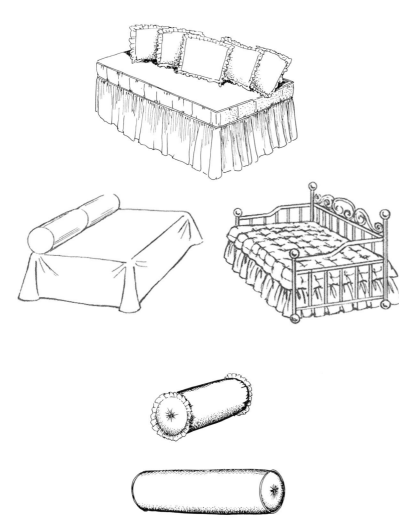

DAYBED COVER

DESCRIPTION:
A fitted twin bedspread with four finished sides and an attached, gathered skirt. The mattress section is quilted with channels or outlining the print. For a more tailored look the skirt can be box pleated.

YARDAGE:
54" fabric, 27" repeat, 11 yds.
48" fabric, no repeat, 13 yds.

WORK ORDER SPECIFICATIONS:
1. Width and length of mattress
2. Depth of mattress
3. Drop from top of mattress to floor
4. Should corners be split?
5. Direction of pattern on bed

SPECIAL NOTE:
To create a more comfortable sitting area, add bolsters and/or cushions. See section on these items.

BOLSTERS

DESCRIPTION:
Neckrolls add a delicate accent to a bed or chaise lounge. Bolsters are the full width of the bed and add extra support for the back and neck. Round bolsters and neckrolls are available with polyester fill for a softer look and feel or foam to create a more structed finish. Wedged bolsters are only available with foam. Used on daybeds, bolsters create a nice seating area.

YARDAGE:
54" fabric, 27" repeat, 11 yds.
48" fabric, no repeat, 13 yds.

YARDAGE:
See chart on the left

WORK ORDER SPECIFICATIONS:
1. Size of neckroll or bolster
2. Details

Neckroll1	1" x 5 1/2" diameter	1 yd.
	14" x 7" diameter	1 yd.
Bolster Twin	39" x 9" diameter	1 1/4 yds.
Double	54" x 9" diameter	1 3/4 yds.
Queen	60" x 9" diameter	2 1/4 yds.
King	78" x 9" diameter	2 1/2 yds.
Wedged Bolster	36" L	1 3/4 yds.
	72" L	3 yds.

PILLOW SHAMS

DESCRIPTION:

A decorative pillow covering which completes the look of a bed when used with a duvet cover or comforter. Ruffles, box ruffles, flanges, piping and ruched piping are some of the extra details that can be used on pillow shams.

YARDAGE:

Pillow Shams (pair)
Standard / Queen   2 1/2 yds.
King   3 1/4 yds.

Details:
Medium Piping   add 1/2 yd.
Jumbo Piping   add 1 yd.
Ruched Piping   add 2 yds.
Flange   add 2 yds.
Cluster Gather   add 2 yds.
3" Ruffle   add 2 1/2 yds.
4" Ruffle   add 3 1/2 yds.
Box Pleated Ruffle   add 3 1/2 yds.

WORK ORDER SPECIFICATIONS:

1. Size of pillow sham
2. Number of pillow shams

SPECIAL NOTE:

Sizes:
Standard 19" x 27"
Queen 20" x 30"
King 20" x 36"

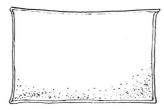

Medium Piping

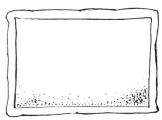

Jumbo Piping

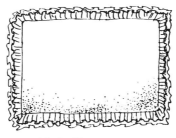

Double Ruffle

Ruched Piping

Pillow Sham with Ruffle

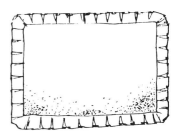

Box Pleated Ruffle

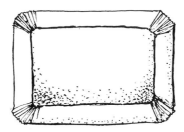

Cluster Gather

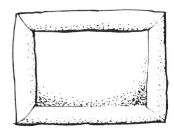

Flange

TOSS CUSHIONS

Piping

Jumbo Piping

Ruched Piping

Ruffle

Double Ruffle

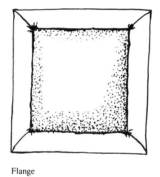

Flange

DESCRIPTION:
Accent your decor with toss cushions. A variety of styles can really add some flavor to a room.

YARDAGE:

	up to 16"	up to 24"
Cushion with		
Regular Piping	3/4 yd.	1 1/2 yds.
For Jumbo Piping	add 3/4 yd.	add 1 yd.
For Ruched Piping	add 1 1/4 yd.	add 2 yds.
For Flanged	add 3/4 yd.	add 1 yd.
For Ruffled	add 1 yd.	add 1 1/2 yds.
For Double Ruffles	add 1 yd.	add 1 1/2 yds.
	each ruffle	each ruffle

WORK ORDER SPECIFICATIONS:
1. Size
2. Shape
3. Style
4. Fabric details

SPECIAL NOTE:
Round cushions are not recommended for knife edge cushions with piping or flanges

DREAM WINDOWS

DREAM WINDOWS

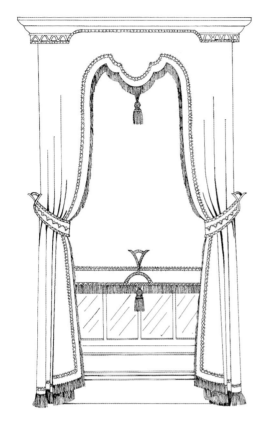

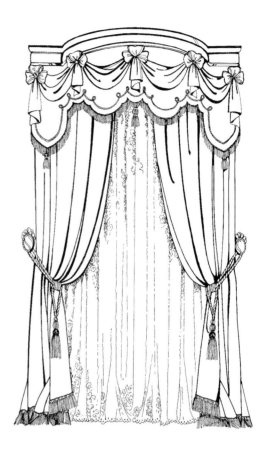

194

DREAM WINDOWS

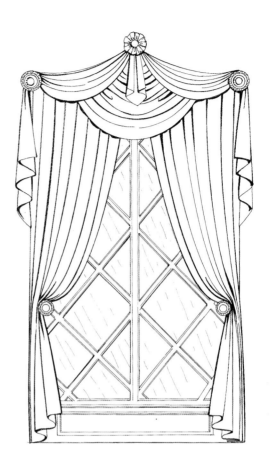

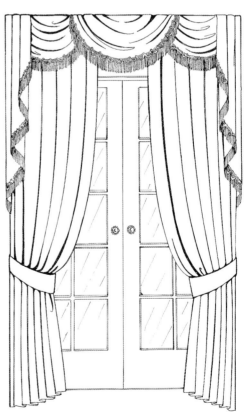

DREAM WINDOWS

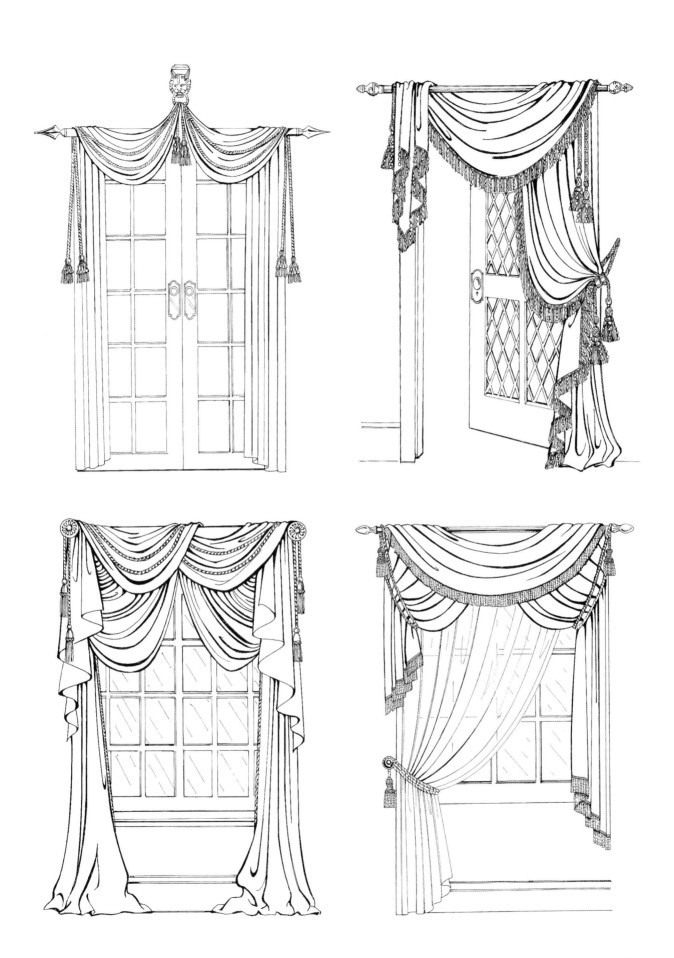

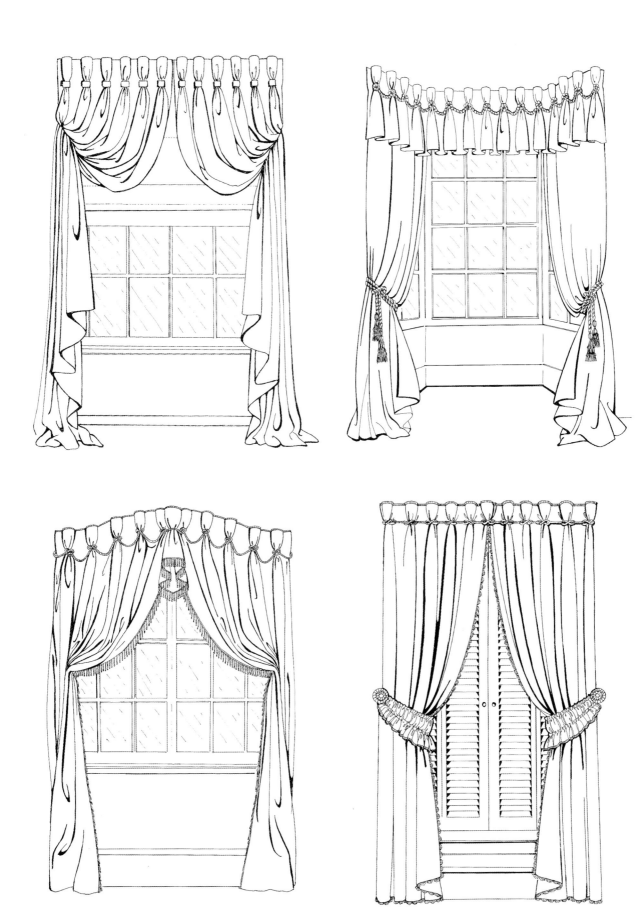

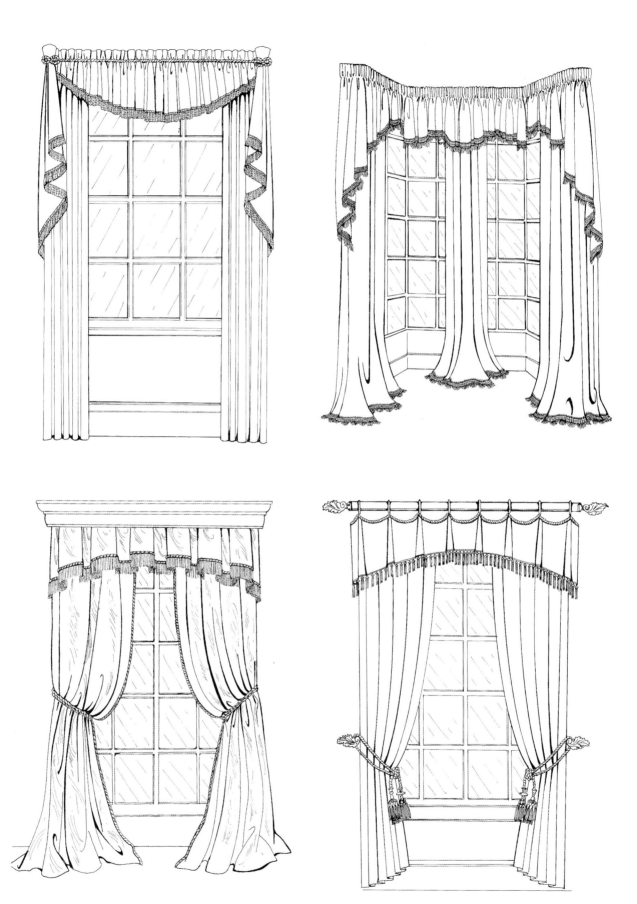

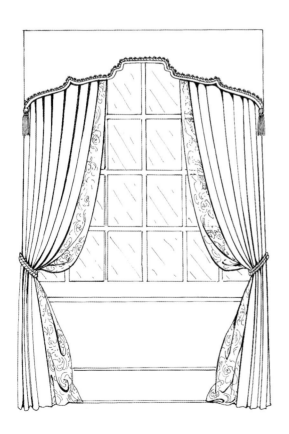

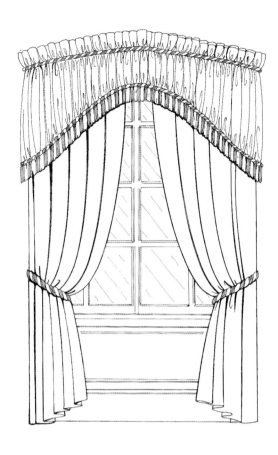

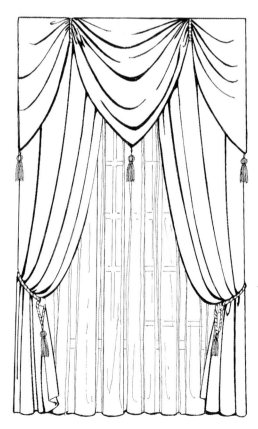

DREAM WINDOWS

Bedding

DREAM WINDOWS

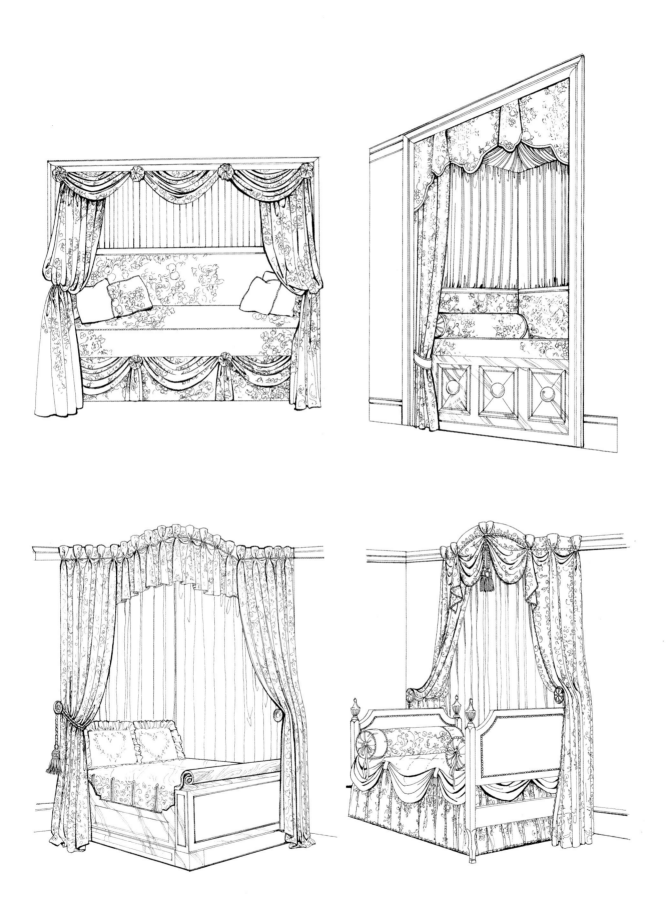

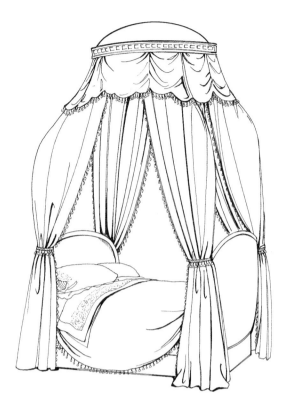

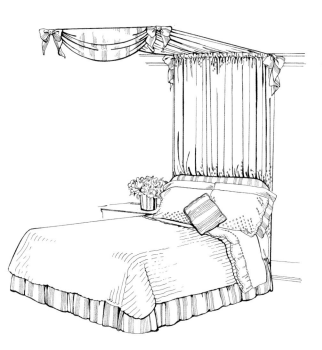

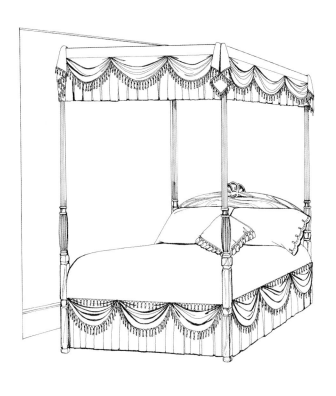

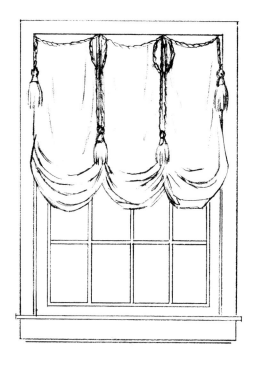

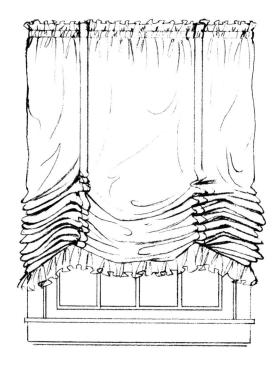

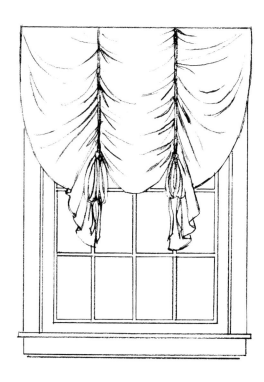

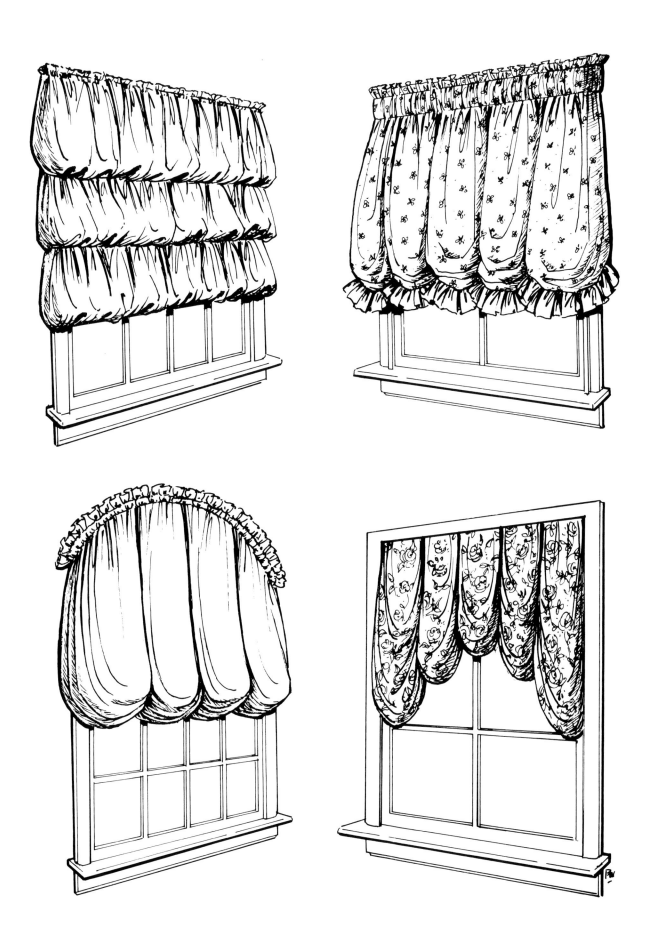

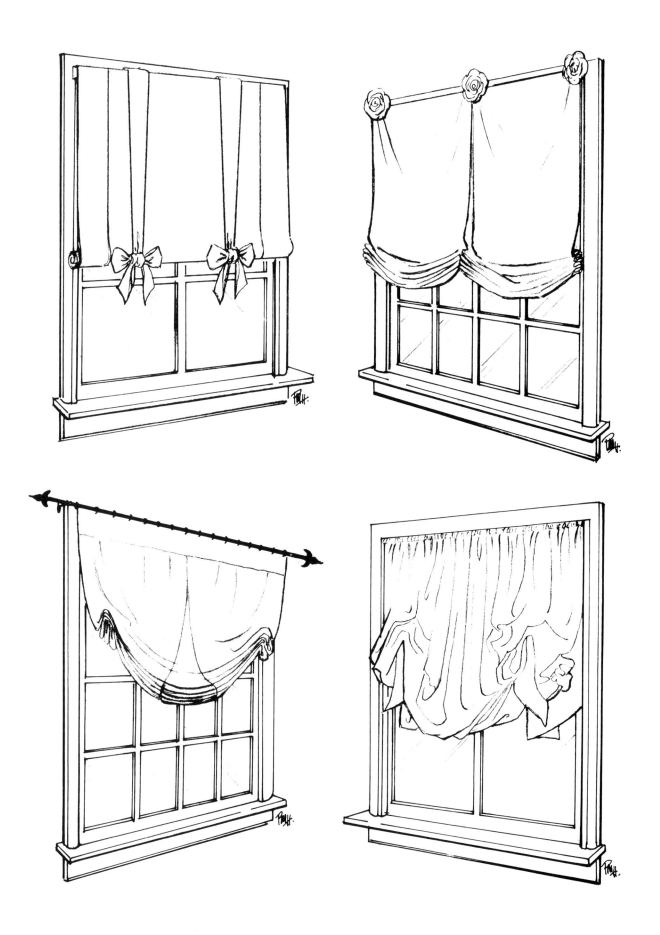

Dream Windows

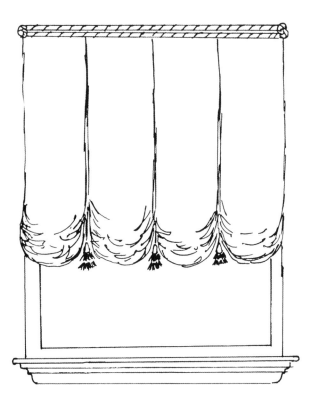

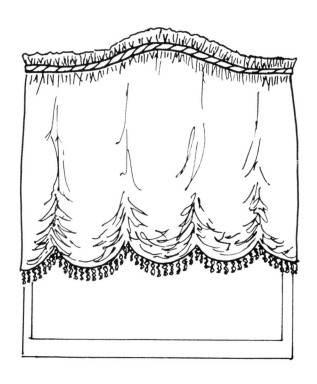

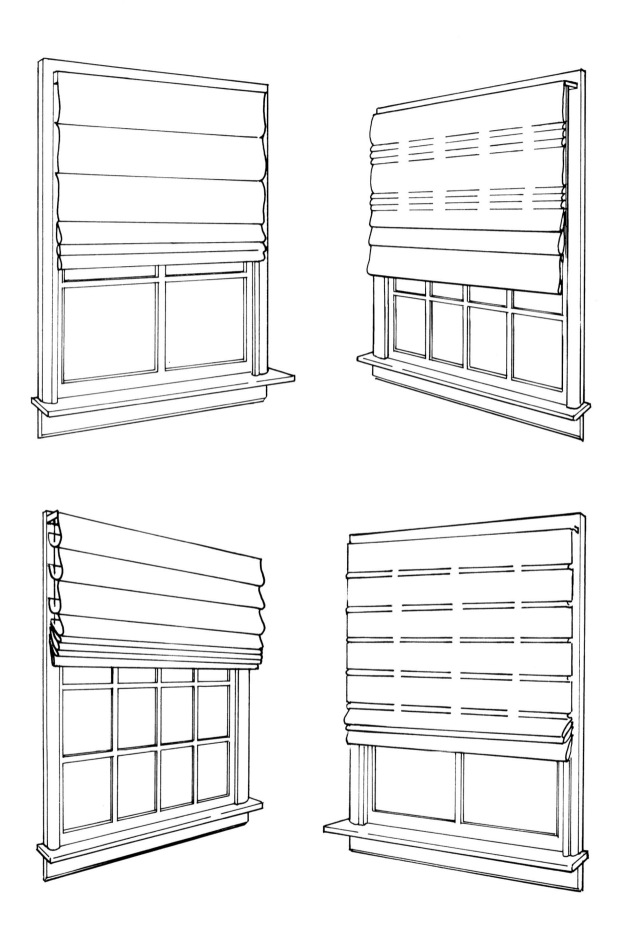

DREAM WINDOWS

GLOSSARY OF DECORATING TERMS

A"A" Frame Window - Very contemporary house structures sometimes form an "A" shape. When draperies are used, they hang from the crossbeam of the "A," or they can be fabricated and installed to conform to the shape of the window.

A La Duchesse - A type of bed supported with a canopy suspension from the ceiling rather than posts. It is also know as an angel bed.

Accordion Pleat - Single large pleats which are often used as a method of fan folding in pleated draperies before installing, or can be used in contract draperies by snapping onto channel slides.

Allowance - A customary variation from an "exact" measurement, taken for the purpose of anticipated needs.

Appliqué - The application of a second, decorated layer of fabric onto a base piece of cloth.

Apron - A piece of wood trim beneath the windowsill.

Architectural Rodding - Used for contract draperies, a sturdy, sleek or traverse channel.

Architrave - The molding around an arch or wooden surrounding to a window or door frame.

Art Deco - A modern, historical design period, which dates from 1909 to 1939.

Art Glass - Glass which is cut at an angle (other than right), stained and etched, and used for hard window treatments.

Art Nouveau - An historical design movement of the Victorian Era, dating from 1890 to 1910. The motifs are based on flowing plant forms.

Asymmetrical Balance - A type of design in which the entire arrangement has a balance, but each side of a central point is different.

Austrian Shade - A shade having ruche down the whole side length, creating billows when the shade is raised.

Automated Exterior Rolling Shutters - A treatment used for insulation and privacy purposes, in which the exterior of a window has metal panels, which roll down mechanically over the glass.

Awning Window - A type of window which can swing out due to a hinged top.

B

Backstitch - A reverse-stitch used to keep the stitches from coming undone at the ends. Several stitches are sewn at the beginning and end of any seam.

Balloon Shade - Shades with vertical rows of horizontally gathered fabric, which can be drawn up to form strips of pleated or gathered trim.

Balloon Tie-backs - Curtains which, when tied back, form a rounded sort of cloud shape.

Bamboo Shade - A natural light-softening shade, drawn by hand using a cord and made of woven panels of split bamboo. Also called a Bali blind.

Baroque - An elaborate interior design period dating from 1643 to 1730 in France and 1660 to 1714 in England.

Bar-Tack - A sewing machine operation of repeated stitches concentrated to secure the lowest portion of drapery pleats.

Basement Windows - Opposite of awning windows, these windows swing inward due to a hinged bottom.

Basting - A technique used in sewing to temporarily fasten layers of fabric using long, loose stitches.

Baton - A rod or wand used to hand draw traverse draperies.

Bay Window - A large projecting type of window made of a group of windows set at angles to each other and joined to each other on some sides.

Bell Valance - A gathered or pleated valance which has a number of bell-like shapes at bottom hemline.

Bias Binding - A strip of fabric used for added strength when binding edges of fabric and closing piping. The fabric is cut in a slanted manner from selvage to selvage.

Bishop's Sleeve Curtains - Tie-back curtains which have been bloused at least two times.

Blind - A hard treatment for a window, consisting of a series of horizontal panels.

Bottom Hem - The turned part forming a finished edge at bottom of drapery.

Bow Window - A large projecting type of window that is curved or semi-circular.

Box Pleat - A fold of cloth sewn into place to create fullness in a drapery. Box pleats are evenly spaced and stitched.

Bracket - Metal piece attached to the wall or casing to support a drapery or curtain rod.

Braid - A woven ribbon which may be used for trimming or can be added to edges of draperies and accessories.

Bull's-Eye Window - A circular window glazed with flat or arched glass.

Butterfly Pleat - A two-part pleat which flares out at the top and is bar-tacked at the bottom.

C

Café - A traversing or non-traversing drapery, designed as a tier. The heading can be various styles. They can be set at a variety of heights to control ventilation, view and light.

Café Rod - A small, round decorative rod which comes in white, brass or woodgrain finish, used to mount café curtains that do not have a rod pocket. Café rods are meant to be seen and add an additional decorative touch to the curtain treatment.

Canopy - A fabric window topper created by sewing pockets into fabric panels and inserting a rod with a small projection at the top of the panel, a rod with a larger projection at the bottom.

Cantonniere - A three-sided shaped or straight cornice that frames a window - across the top and down the two sides. Made of a hardboard, padded and covered with fabric.

Cape Cod Curtain - A café curtain decorated by a ruffle around the bottom and sides. This is also called a ruffle-round curtain.

Carriers - Small runners installed in a traverse rod which hold a drapery pin or hook.

Cartridge Pleat - A fold of cloth sewn into place to create fullness in a drapery. This is a round pleat 2-2 1/2 inches in depth. Roundness is created by stuffing crinoline or paper (removed for cleaning).

Cascade - A fall of fabric that descends in a zigzag line from a drapery heading or top treatment.

Cased Heading - A curtain heading with a simple, hemmed top, in which a rod is inserted.

Casement - (1) A cloth drapery that is of an open-weave material but more opaque than a sheer. (2) A type of vertically hinged window, whose panes open by sliding sideways or cranking outward.

Casing (Window) - Wooden frame around a window.

Catchstitch - A stitch used for hemming raw edges, and then covered by a piece of fabric.

Cathedral Window - A window which points upward, and is formed at an angle.

Center Draw - One pair of draperies which draws open and closes exactly at a window's center point.

Center Support - A metal grip which is used to support a traverse rod from above and prevents rod form sagging in the middle, but does not interfere with rod operation.

Clerestory Windows - A series of small windows which let in light and air. These are placed high on the wall to allow complete privacy.

Colonial - A design period common prior to the revolutionary war in America. It is typically dated from 1608 to 1790.

Corbel Bay - A second story bay window.

Cord - A cable yarn which can be made from either cotton or synthetic materials. It is used for various reasons including holding blinds and shades together, and as a means for drawing traverse draperies, shades and blinds.

Corner Window - A corner window that wraps a corner of the building at right angles.

Cornice - A shallow, box-like structure, usually made of wood, fastened across the top of a window to conceal the drapery hardware.

Cornice Board - A horizontal board used as support for a cornice or as foundation for swags and tails.

Cornice Pole - A curtain pole having rings and used for heavy curtains.

Corona Drape - A drapery which is hung at the top of a bed from a semi-circular bracket or a pole.

Cottage Curtains - A term used to describe curtains displayed in a casual or informal manner.

Country Curtains - A casual curtain treatment with ruffles at valance, bottom, sides and ties. The curtain is shirred a maximum of five times in fullness and is usually made with plain or tiny-printed fabric.

Coverage - A term used to describe the fullness of fabric used on a window.

Crown Glass - A particular type of glass consisting of hand-blown crowns, measuring about one meter in diameter.

Curtain - A window covering either hung from rings, or made with a casing so that it slips over a rod. Curtains are informal window coverings.

Custom Glazing - Unusual sized or oddly shaped window glass, which is custom made and installed.

Custom-Made Draperies - Draperies made to order in a workroom or decorator shop.

Cut Length - The length after allowances have been made for heading and hem.

Cut Width - The width that the fabric should be cut after allowances have been made.

D

Decorator Rods - Hardware used for the purpose of decorating, that is meant to be seen in the open. Usually made from chrome, wood, brass or antique wrought iron.

Diaphanous Sheers - Drapery used for the purpose of daytime privacy. The finely woven transparent fabrics filter out glare. Also know as glass curtains.

Dormer Window - An upright window which breaks the surface of a sloping roof.

Double Hung - May be several items: Double-hung window, Double-hung shutters or Double-hung draperies (two sets of Draperies, usually sheer fabric under opaque fabric, both operating independently).

Drapability - How well a fabric can flow or fall into folds in an attractive manner.

Drapery - A window covering which is usually hung from a traverse rod. Draperies most often have pleated headings which may be lined or unlined.

Draw Draperies - Panels of fabric, featuring pleated headings.

Dress Curtains - Curtains used for the sole purpose of decorating. They are not meant to be drawn.

E

Ease - Refers to extra fabric allowance given in order to make the finished length more accurate. Sometimes fabric that was not calculated into the final length will be lost when stitching double - fold hems, headings or rod pockets, or when gathering a treatment onto a rod. It is a good idea to add 1/2" ease to the length before cutting to ensure a more accurate finish.

Elements of Design - The elements which make up a design, including: texture, light, color, space, form, shape, pattern and ornament.

Empire - A design period dating from 1804 to 1820 in France and 1820 to 1860 in America.

End Bracket - The two supporting metal grips which hold a drapery rod to the wall or ceiling. They control the amount of projection.

End Housing - Refers to the box parts at the extreme ends of a traverse drapery rod. They enclose the mechanism through which the cords run.

End Pleat - The final pleat in a drapery, hooked into the end bracket.

English Sash Window - A sliding frame consisting of a number of rectangular shaped glass panels. Also called Renaissance sash.

F

Fabric Finishes - Treatments used to give the fabric more durability, decoration and usefulness. These can be chemical or mechanical.

Fabric Sliding Panels - Panels of fabric which are drawn with a baton. They are flat, overlapping and installed on a track rod.

Face Fabric - The primary fabric on draperies or curtains. This is the fabric which faces the interior of the room.

Facing - A strip of fabric over the main fabric, with the purpose of hiding raw edges and unlined curtains or draperies.

Factory-Made Treatments - Custom specifications in hard window treatments ordered from a manufacturer or factory. These include shades, shutters, blinds and screens.

Fan Folding - Fan folding helps to obliterate wrinkling, set the folds and give better drapability. This is done by folding pleated draperies into a thin band.

Fascia - A rectangular-shaped board set horizontally with the purpose of covering a curtain heading or shade fixture.

Federal Period - A design period dating from 1790 to 1820. Also called Neoclassic.

Fenestration - Location and proportion of windows in relationship to solid wall areas.

Festoon - A decorative drapery treatment of folded fabric that hangs in a graceful curve and frames the top of a window. Also called Parisian shade.

Finial - Decorative end piece on café rods or decorative traverse Rods. Also referred to as pole ends.

Finished Length - The length after draperies have been made, using the extra allowances in hem and heading.

Finished Width - The width after draperies have been made. Found by measuring the length of the mounting board or rod and then adding in the depth of any returns.

Fixed Glass - Term used to describe windows which are not made to open or close.

Flat Curtain Rod - A curtain rod that differs from a traverse rod in that it does not use a pulley and cord to operate.

Flemish Heading - A goblet type of heading where each of the pleats are connected along their base using a hand-sewn cord.

Flounce - A technique adding an extra long heading sewn at the top of a rod pocket and having the curtain fall over the rod pocket to create the appearance of a short, attached valance.

French Door Draw - A swinging door or casement window with one-way traverse rods attached.

French Doors - Doors in a pair, which are lengthwise, mostly made up of glass panes.

French Pleats - A three-fold pleat; one of the most used pleats in draperies.

French Seam - A seam most often used when the seam will be visible, or when using lightweight fabrics.

Fringe - An edging with hanging tassels or threads, used as decoration.

Fullness - The proportion of the finished width of the valance or curtain to the length of the mounting board or rod.

G

Gathered Heading - A heading for a curtain or valance in which the heading is gathered by means of gathering tape.

Gathering Tape - A tape stitched to the top of a curtain to create a gathered effect by pulling on cords which run through the tape.

Gathers - Folding and puckering formed when pulling on loosely-stitched thread.

Georgian Period - A design period which dates from 1700 to 1790.

Glue-Baste - A technique using glue to secure two pieces of fabric together before sewing.

Goblet Heading - A curtain heading having a series of hand-sewn tubes, in which each of the tops are stuffed with padding or contrast fabric.

Goblet Pleats - Similar to pinch pleats, except that the top edge is padded and pushed out in a goblet type of shape.

Greenhouse Window - A window that generally extends at a 90-degree angle from the wall, has a glass top and sides and two accompanying shelves for plants.

Group Pleat - A set of pleats, generally three, with space between each one.

H

Half-Canopy - A canopy above a bed in a rectangular shape, which extends only partially from the headboard down the bed.

Heading - The hemmed, usually stiffened, portion across the top of a curtain or drapery.

Hem - Refers to finished sides and bottom edges of a drapery.

Holdback - A decorative piece of hardware that holds

draperies to each side of the window.

I

Insert Pulley - An auxiliary traverse rod part, over which the cords operate.

Inside Mount - A treatment installed inside of a window frame.

Installation - A process which undergoes the various aspects of placing and setting a window treatment.

Interlining - A fabric, usually of soft material, sewn in between the curtain and the back lining to improve bulk, insulation and overall drapability.

Inverted Pleat - A pleat formed the opposite way of a traditional box pleat, in which the edges of the pleat meet in the middle right side of the fabric. Also know as the kick pleat.

J

Jabot – The decorative, vertical end of an over treatment that usually finishes a horizontal festoon.

Jalousie Window - A window made from a number of horizontal slants, delivering good ventilation properties.

Jamb - Interior sides of a door or window frame.

K

Keystone Arch - An arch used as part of a wooden molding for decoration, rounded and Roman in style.

Knife Pleats - Narrow, finely pressed and closely spaced pleats which all go in the same direction.

L

Lambrequin - A cornice that completely frames the window. Sometimes used interchangeably with valance or cantonniere.

Laminated Weights - Weight covered on both sides to avoid rust marks on draperies.

Lanai - A type of window covering made of a series of hinged, rigid plastic panels, hung from a traverse track.

Lapped Seam - A seam, which is most useful for matching patterns together on the right sides of two separate pieces of fabric.

Lining - A fabric backing for a drapery.

Lintel - Wood, steel or reinforced concrete beams placed over both window and door openings to hold up the wall and roof above.

Lit a la Polonnaise - A drape set made to fall from a center point above a bed.

Lock Stitch - A stitch purposely made loose, to give way for a little movement. An excellent stitch when used for holding together fabrics, linings and interlinings.

Louvers – Slats, generally made from metal, wood or plastic. These can be horizontal or vertical and are used for blinds and shutters.

M

Master Carrier - Two arms that overlap in the center of a rod when draperies are closed, allowing them to close completely.

Milium - Trade name for a thermal lining.

Miniblinds - A series of one-inch, horizontal metal or plastic slats, which are held together with a cord. They can be tilted and lifted. Micro-miniblinds are similar except that the slats are only a 1/2 inch.

Miter - A technique in folding the fabric so as to keep excess fabric out of sight, eliminating bulk.

Mitered Corner - The formation of the bottom edge of a drapery with a 45-degree angle on hem side.

Modern Period - A design period dating from 1900 to present.

Mullion - The vertical wood or masonry sections between a series of window frames.

Multi-Draw – The simultaneous opening and closing of several draperies on one rod at one time.

Muntin - The horizontal wooden strips that separate panes of glass in windows.

N

Neoclassic Period - A design period dating from 1760 to 1789 in France, 1770 to 1820 in England and 1790 to 1820 in America.

Notch - A tiny cut, usually in a V-shape, at the edge of a fabric.

O

Off-Center - A window not centered on a wall, but draperies still meet at its center point.

One-Way Draw - Drapery designed to draw only one way, in one panel.

Opacity - A degree measuring the amount to which solid material blocks view and light.

Open Cuff - On the backside of a drapery and at top. Open cuffs make one of the strongest type headings on any drapery. This results when you carry both fabrics to the top and make a turn with the crinoline.

Oriel Bay - Similar to a corbel bay window, but having the second story window descend down to the first floor.

Orientation - A term used to describe the direction in which a window faces: north, east, south or west.

Outside Mount - A treatment installed over and to the side of a window frame on the wall.

Overdraperies - A layer of drapery fabric which is installed over an existing layer of drapery.

Overlap - The part of a drapery panel, which rides the master carrier of a traverse rod, and overlaps in the center when draperies are drawn closed, usually 3 1/2” on each side.

P

Padded Edge - A fabric border rolled and stuffed to form a Long, round shape.

Palladian Window - A window consisting of a high, rounded, middle section and two lower squared sections at each side. Also know as a Venetian Window.

Panel - One half of a pair of draperies or curtains.

Passementerie - This term is used to describe the vast range of trimmings and decorative edges.

Pattern Repeat - The distance between any given point in a design to where that exact point is repeated again.

Pelmet - A upholstered wood cornice or stiffened and shaped valance.

Pencil-Pleat Heading - Formed by a certain type of tape that, when pulled together, creates a column of tightly-packed folds.

Period Window Treatment - Refers to historically designed treatments from any specific design period.

Picture Window - A type of window with a large center glass area with two smaller glass areas on each side.

Pinch Pleats - A drapery heading where the basic pleat is divided into two or three smaller, equal pleats, sewn together at the bottom edge on the right side of the fabric.

Pin-On-Hook - A metal pin to fasten draperies to a rod. It pins into drapery pleats and hooks to traverse carrier or café rod.

Piping - Cords used at the edges of a curtain for added affects, usually fabric covered and put in through a seam.

Pivot - While sewing corners, this technique has one stop the machine with the needle down in the fabric, and then turn the fabric at the corner before continuing to stitch.

Plate Glass - A design which was popular in France from the Seventeenth century to the nineteenth century. Molten glass is ironed smooth after being poured onto a table, and is then made into large sheets.

Pleat - A fold of cloth sewn into place to create fullness.

Pleat To - The finished width of the fabric after it has been pleated. Example: A width of 48” fabric has been pleated to 18” - “Pleat To” 18”.

Pleater Tape - Pocketed heading material designed to be used with pleating hooks.

Polonnaise - A bed set against the wall lengthwise, having a small, ascending dome.

Portiere - A term used to describe a doorway treatment, either a hung curtain or drapery.

Pouf Shade - Shades or valances with a soft-looking fabric and a gathered hem.

Pressing - An important part of sewing technique. With an iron selected to the appropriate setting for a particular fabric, a steaming method is used by lifting the iron up and pressing it down, instead of sliding it across the fabric.

Principles of Design - The theory of design made possible by manipulating the elements of design to create proper balance, emphasis, proportion and scale.

Priscilla Curtains - Curtains with ruffled valance, sides, bottom, hem and ties. They are usually made from sheer or opaque fabrics and sometimes they meet or cross in the center.

Projection - Refers to a jutting out, an extension. On a curtain or drapery rod, it is that part which returns to the wall from the front of the rod.

Protractor - A drapery tool by which exact angles are measured (as in bay windows).

R

Railroading - Some decorator fabrics use railroading in correspondence to widths for floor-length treatments. In this technique the lengthwise grain runs in a horizontal manner across the window treatment, making vertical seams unnecessary.

Ready-Mades - Standard size draperies, factory-made and available at local stores or through mail-order sources.

Renaissance Period - A design period dating from 1400 to 1600 in Italy, 1589 to 1643 in France and 1558 to 1649 in England. An era rich in art, literature, architecture and science.

Repeat - The space from one design motif to the next on a patterned fabric.

Return - The distance from the face of the rod to the wall of the casing where the bracket is attached.

Reveals - Sides to a window opening, with right angles facing the wall and window.

Rococo Period - A French design period dating from 1730 to 1760, where decorations were curved, asymmetrical and ornamental.

Rod - A metal or plastic device from which curtains are hung, an alternative to a pole. Double rods are used for two layers of fabric.

Rod Pocket - A hollow sleeve in the top - and sometimes the bottom - of a curtain or drapery through which a rod is inserted. The rod is then attached to a solid wall surface.

Rod Width - Measures the width between the end of a bracket to the end of the other bracket including the stackback and window width.

Roller Shade - A shade operated by a device with a spring. When the spring is let loose, the shade coils itself around the device's cylinder.

Roman Shade - A corded shade with rods set horizontally in back to give the shade a number of neat side-set pleats or folds when raised.

RTB - Rod top and bottom.

Ruching - A thin area of pleated or gathered fabric, often used for trimming or tie-backs.

Ruffle - A decorative trimming consisting of a strip of gathered fabric.

R-Value - A window treatment, ceiling or wall's capacity to keep heat in or out.

S

Sash - A wooden frame used to hold the glass of swinging and sliding windows.

Sash Curtain - Any sheer material hung close to the window glass. Usually hung from spring tension rods or sash rods mounted inside the window casing.

Sash Rod - A small rod, either decorative or plain, usually mounted inside a window frame on the sash.

Scalloped Heading - A popular top treatment for café curtains featuring semi-circular spaces between curtain rings.

Seam - Stitching two pieces of fabric together at the right sides, leaving the stitches hidden on the other side of the fabric, for a clean, finished look on the right side.

Seam Allowance - A slim, extra allowance in the fabric between the line for stitching and the raw edge of the fabric.

Selvedge - The tightly woven edge on a width of fabric to hold the fabric together.

Shade - A window covering usually made from cloth or vinyl that covers the glass, and rolls up or down off of the window.

Sheet Glass - Popular in the 21st century, large sheets of glass are created by casting or drawing and then used for glazing.

Shirring - A rod that is smaller than the fabric width is slid through a rod pocket to create a gathered effect in the fabric.

Shoji Screen - An oriental design with paper attached to a wooden grid, forming a translucent effect with sliding or stationary panels.

Shutters - A series of folding wooden panels, which are hung by a side hinge.

Side Hem - The turned part forming a finished edge at the side of the drapery.

Sill - The horizontal "ledge-like" portion of a window casing.

Skylights - A window set into a ceiling or roof, made from glass or plastic.

Slides - Small runners installed in a traverse rod which hold a drapery pin or hook.

Slip Stitch - Matching colored thread is used to stitch the folded edge of a lining to the base fabric.

Smocked Heading - A curtain heading consisting of a honeycomb effect. A heading full of pencil pleats hooked together at specific spacing give this effect.

Spacing - Refers to the flat space between pleats; the fuller the drapery, the less the spacing.

Spanish Arch - A rounded arch designed in Spanish fashion.

Stacking - The area required for draperies when they are completely open. Also referred to as stackback.

Swag - A section of draped fabric above a window.

T

Tails - Shaped and stiffened or free falling, hanging trails of fabric from the end of swags.

Tambour Curtains - Curtains that originally were used as folk craft in Scandinavia, they are lightweight or sheer embroidered fabrics.

Tape-Gathered Heading - A gathered effect for curtain headings, using thin threaded tape sewn onto the top of a curtain and then pulled by the parallel threads.

Tension Pulley - The pulley attachment through which the traverse cords move for one continuous smooth operation when a drapery is drawn. May be mounted on a baseboard, casing or wall, on one or both sides.

Tester - A canopy supported by a bed with tall corner posts.

Tie - A thin strip of fabric which is used with tie-backs to secure a drapery to a wall. The tie can be decorated or shaped.

Tie-backs - Decorative pieces of hardware, sometimes called holdbacks. Available in many forms and designed to hold draperies back from the window to allow light passage or add an additional decorative touch to the window treatment.

Tier - Curtain layers arranged one above the other with a normal overlap of 4". Upper tiers project from the wall at a greater distance than lower panels to allow each curtain to hang free.

Traverse - To draw across. A traverse drapery is one that opens or closes across a window by means of the traverse rod from which it is hung.

Traverse Rod - A rod which is operated by a cord and pulley.

Turkish Bed - A thin bed set back into a draped alcove.

U

Under-Draperies - A lightweight drapery, usually a sheer, closest to the window glass. It hangs beneath a heavier over-drapery.

V

Valance - A horizontal decorative fabric treatment used at the top of draperies to screen hardware and cords.

Victorian - A design period dating from 1837 to 1910 in England and 1840 to 1920 in America.

W

Wall Fasteners - Window treatments are fastened to hollow walls using toggle bolts or molly bolts.

Weave - The act of interlacing when forming a piece of fabric.

Weights - Lead weights are sewn into the vertical seams and corners of a drapery panel. Chain weights are small beads, strung in a line along the bottom hemline of sheers, to insure an even hemline and straight hanging.

Width - A word to describe a single width of fabric. Several widths of fabric are sewn together to make a panel of drapery.

Z

Zigzag Stitch - One of various sewing machine settings. In this Stitch, the needle moves back and forth, at the desired length and width, in a zigzag pattern. This stitch is often used for finishing seams.

GLOSSARY OF FABRIC TERMS

A

Acetate - Used to make many persuasive artificial silks. It has similar draping and finish qualities to silk but is less likely to rot or fade.

Acrylic - A soft lightweight fabric made from a synthetic longchain polymer, primarily made of acrylonitrile.

Aluminum-Coated - A lining used to help exclude light, heat and cold. It is not visible, as it faces inside the fabric, while the outside of the fabric shows woven cream cotton.

Antique Satin - One of the most common drapery fabrics sold. Characterized by a lustrous effect, normally composed of rayon/acetate blends.

B

Baize - Similar to flannel and dyed green or red. Mostly used for card tables or lining silverware drawers. Its texture and color make it convenient for improvised shades or curtains. Fades in sunlight.

Basketweave - Plain under-and-over weave; primarily in draperies.

Batik - A dyeing technique developed in Java, where dye is applied and then washed, leaving bold patterns.

Batiste - A soft finished fabric, which has a high count of fine yarns. It is more opaque than voiles. Usually composed of 100% polyester or a polyester blend.

Batting - A man-made fluffy fiber, used for padding edges.

Bias - A diagonal line which intersects the crosswise and lengthwise grain of any fabric. Woven fabrics, which do not stretch at the crosswise or lengthwise grains, do stretch at the bias.

Blackout - A heavy interlining in which a layer of opaque material is placed between two pieces of cotton to block out any light. Improves the drapability qualities. It is most often white or cream.

Boucle - French for curled, indicates a curled or looped surface.

Broadcloth - (1) A medium to heavyweight twill blend or worsted wool fabric which is napped and felted. (2) A cotton fabric similar to muslin, due to its fine crosswise cords.

Brocade - Rich jacquard - woven fabric with all-over interwoven design of raised figures or flowers. Brocade has a raised surface in contrast to felt damask, and is generally made of silk, rayon and nylon yarns with or without metallic treatment.

Brocatelle - Usually made of silk or wool, similar to brocades.

Bump - Interlining imported from England, heavy weight, cotton, and available bleached or unbleached. Similar to table felt and reinforcement felt, but slightly stiffer. Cotton flannel is often used instead of bump.

Burlap - Coarse, canvas-like fabric made of jute, hemp or cotton. Also called Gunny.

C

Canvas - A heavy woven cotton and linen blend, similar to cotton duck.

Casements – Open-weave casual fabric, characterized by its instability.

Challis - One of the softest fabrics made. Normally made of rayon and sometimes combined with cotton.

Cheesecloth - Cheap and loosely woven, this fabric will easily fade, wrinkle and shrink. Similar to muslin.

Chiffon - A transparent sheer fabric with a soft finish.

Chintz - Glazed cotton fabric often printed with bright colors or large, floral designs. Some glazes will wash out in laundering. The only durable glaze is a resin finish which will withstand washing or dry cleaning. Unglazed chintz is called cretonne.

Corduroy - A cut-filling pile cloth with narrow to wide wales which run in the warp direction of the goods and made possible by the use of an extra set of filling yarns in the construction. The back is of plain or twill weave, the latter affording the better construction. Washable types are available and stretch and durable press garments of corduroy are very popular. Usually an all-cotton cloth, some corduroy is now made with nylon or rayon pile effect on a cotton backing fabric or with polyester-cotton blends.

Cotton - An inexpensive, versatile fiber which can be printed, dyed and finished in numerous ways. It also has the ability to be made colorfast and withstand light and heat. It is popular among furnishing fabrics when used alone or as a cotton blend. Its shortcomings include crushing and mildewing.

Cotton Duck - A cotton varying in weight from 7 to 15 oz. per yard. Heavier types are ideal for no-sew curtains as lining is unnecessary and the edges can be glued or pinked.

Cotton Lawn - Finely woven cotton, given an extremely smooth finish.

Crash - A coarse fabric having a rough, irregular surface obtained by weaving thick, uneven yarns. Usually cotton or linen, sometimes spun rayon or blends.

Cretonne - A cotton fabric usually having printed floral or angular shapes. It is a plain weave, unglazed and coarser than chintz.

Crewelwork - Indian Cotton, wool or linen fabric adorned with wool chain stitching. Most often on a cream background. Used as early American and English bed hangings.

Crinoline - A heavily-sized, stiff fabric used as a foundation to support the edge of a hem or puffed sleeve. Can be used as interlining. Also referred to as Buckram.

Crosswise Grain - Crosswise grain runs perpendicular to the selvages on woven fabric.

D

Dacron - A synthetic fiber with good filling and padding qualities.

Damask - Firm, glossy jacquard-patterned fabric. Similar to brocade but flatter and reversible. Can be made from linen, cotton, rayon or silk, or a combination of fibers.

Denim - A sturdy fabric, mostly in dark blue, twill weave. Also called jean.

Domette - A lightweight cotton interlining imported from England. Similar to American needle-punched fleece. It is used with light shades, curtains and swags.

Dotted Swiss - A sheer fabric with opaque dots, sometimes given a raised texture.

Double Knit - A fabric knitted with a double stitch on a double needle frame to provide a double thickness and is the same on both sides. Has excellent body and stability.

Dupion - Textured, real or synthetic silk. It is lightweight, which gives this fabric the tendency to rot or fade. Synthetic dupion is made from viscose and acetate and real silk dupion is typically imported from India.

E

Eyelet - Embroidered white cotton fabric often used for unlined shades or light curtains.

F

Fabric Identification Label - This label will tell the fiber content, width and care method for the fabric, and sometimes the pattern repeat. The fabric identification label is found on the bolt or tube of fabric.

Faille - Plain weave (flat-rib); with filling yarns heavier than warp.

Figured Material - A fabric whose pattern is created from the structure of the weave.

Foamback - Term used to denote that a fabric has been laminated to a backing of polyurethane foam.

Fusible Buckram - A strip of white cotton filled with glue and used as a stiffener. Good for use inside of hand-pleated headings to avoid the visibility of machine stitching. It is fused to the fabric with a hot iron.

Fusible Heavyweight Buckram - An open-weave stiffener, made from jute and filled with glue. It is used for the base of a cornice. A hot iron will fuse it in place, releasing the glue.

G

Gauze - A sheer but coarse fabric, available in a variety of thread thicknesses.

Gimp - A wind of fabric which can be stiffened with wire or cord.

Gingham - A cheap, classic cotton fabric with a checkered pattern. The checkers come in a variety of sizes and mostly primary colors.

Glassing - Thin finish provides luster, sheen, shine or polish to some fabrics. Chintz is an example of a glazed fabric.

Grosgrain - A silk fabric with a ribbed texture on surface.

H

Hand, Handle - The reaction of the sense of touch when fabrics are held in the hand. There are many factors which give "character or individuality" to a material observed through handling. A correct judgment may thus be made concerning its capabilities in content, working properties, drapability, feel, elasticity, fineness and softness, launderability, etc.

Herringbone - A versatile medium weight fabric with a zigzag pattern, named after the spine of the herring fish. It is a novelty twill weave, available mostly in neutral colors. Also called Chevron.

Holland - A linen or cotton medium-weight fabric, fade resistant and sturdy, also stiffened with oil or shellac. Standard for valances and roller shades due to its non-fraying edges.

I

Ikat - Chinese cotton or silk fabric with faint geometric patterns as a result of tie dying.

Inherent Flame Frees - Fabric woven of from unprocessed, flame-resistant material and flame-free for life of the fabric.

Interfacing - A fabric stiffener used to give support and hold the shape of the fabric.

J

Jacquard - A loom which can produce woven patterns in a variety of colors. The patterns are known for being intricate and large.

Jute - An inexpensive, easily available and long lasting fabric. Comes in a neutral color but can be dyed. Like linen, it is one of the most important fabrics.

K

Khaki - A beige or earth toned, plain or twill weave fabric with a wide range of uses.

L

Lace - Openwork fabric, generally made from cotton, created by twisting and knotting threads against a net-like background to form the desired design. Lace has an endless variety of designs and is convenient for glass curtains.

Lengthwise Grain - Runs parallel to the selvages on woven fabric. Fabrics are typically stronger along the lengthwise grain.

Linen - A product of the flax plant. Linen possesses rapid moisture absorption, a neutral luster and stiffness and will not soil quickly.

Linen Union – A cotton-linen blend fabric, durable and reasonably priced.

M

Madras Cotton - Inexpensive Indian cotton, woven in a checkered, plaid or striped fashion and brightly colored. Sometimes referred to as sari fabric.

Marquisette - An open mesh, thin fabric. Usually made from synthetic fibers.

Matelasse - Appearance of a quilted weave; figured pattern with a raised, bubbly surface.

Mesh - A term used to describe textiles or open-weave fabrics having a net-like structure.

Modacrylic - A modified fiber in which the fiber-forming substance of any long-chain synthetic polymer is composed of less than 85%, but at least 25%, acrylonitrile units.

Mohair - Comes from the Angora goat. It is lighter weight drapery fabric with a slightly brushed or hairy finish.

Moiré - A finish-given cotton, silk, acetate, rayon, nylon, etc., where bright and dim effects are observed. This is achieved by passing the fabric between engraved rollers which press the particular motif into the fabric.

Moreen - A heavyweight fabric in a wool or wool and cotton blend fabric, usually having a watered pattern.

Muslin - Usually white or off-white in color, this fabric is sheer and delicately woven, but strong.

N

Ninon - A smooth, transparent, high-textured type of voile fabric. Usually made from 100% polyester.

Non-Fusible Buckram - A medium-weight cotton stiffener, typically sewn into tie-backs.

Non-Fusible Heavyweight Buckram - Two-ply double starched stiffener made from jute; unlike fusible heavyweight buckram, it is sewn onto the cornice instead of being fused. It is also easier to clean than the fusible version.

Nylon - A durable and versatile fabric, made from a long-chain polymer, originating from petroleum, air, natural gas and water. It has remarkable strength and is moderately priced.

O

Olefin - A wax-like fiber, made from petroleum products. It is lightweight but strong, and inexpensive.

Ombre - A graduate or shade effect of color used in a striped motif. Usually ranges from light to dark tones. Also called jaspe or strie.

Organdy - Very light and thin, transparent, stiff and wiry cotton cloth. Its crispness will withstand repeated launderings Organdy is a true, durable finish cloth.

P

Padding - A soft and bulky fabric used for stuffing or filling.

Paisley - A timeless motif, this fine woolen cloth has detailed pine, floral or scroll-type designs printed or woven onto it.

Plaid - A fabric which can be printed or woven with rectangular and square shapes in a variety of colors.

Plush - A favorite of the Victorian era, this fabric is an old-fashioned form of velvet made from wool, mohair, and less often cotton, with a deeper but more thinly scattered pile. Now in modern times, it is man made.

Polyester - A stable fabric which displays excellent drapability. This fabric can be woven or knit.

Poplin - Sometimes printed decoratively, this is a plain weave with raised, circular weft cords created with large filling threads. Can be cotton, blend or synthetic and has a variety of uses.

R

Raw Edge - The edge of fabric which is cut, having neither selvage nor hem.

Rayon - Displays a texture similar to silk in touch and visibility. Rayon is available in a vast range of textures and types.

Repp - A fabric having ribbed qualities or appearance.

S

Saran - A plastic, vinyl fiber, durable and colorfast.

Sateen - A firmly woven, strong cotton or cotton blend fabric, usually having stripes or bright solid colors. The finish is smooth and shiny.

Satin Weave - One of the three basic weaves, the others being plain and twill. The surface of satin weave cloth is made almost entirely of warp or filling floats since, in the repeat of the weave, each yarn of one system passes or floats over or under all but one yarn of the opposite system. Satin weaves have a host of uses including brocade, brocatelle and damask.

Selvage - Each side edge of a woven fabric and an actual part of the warp in the goods. Other names for it are listing, self edge, and raw edge.

Shantung - An inconsistently textured raw silk, once hand-woven in China's Shantung Province.

Silk - The only natural fiber that comes in a filament form, reeled from the cocoon, cultivated or wild.

Slub Yarn - Yarn of any type which is irregular in diameter. May be caused by error, or may purposely be made with slubs to bring out a desired effect.

Suede Cloth - A fabric made to be similar to suede leather in visibility and touch.

T

Taffeta - A fine, plain weave fabric that is smooth on both sides, usually with a sheen on its surface.

Tapestry - A heavy, well insulating fabric, once made in replication of hand-sewn tapestries, but now produced on a jacquard loom.

Tartan - A cloth fabric made of a specific checkered pattern, having particular colors of a certain Scottish clan. This fabric has great insulating qualities.

Terry Cloth - This cloth fabric has uncut loops on both sides of the cloth. Terry is also made on a jacquard loom to form interesting motifs.

Texture - (1) The actual number of warp threads and filling picks per inch in any cloth that has been woven. (2) The finish and appearance of cloth.

Thread Count - (1) The actual number of warp ends and filling picks per inch in a woven cloth, also known as texture. (2) In knitted fabric, thread count implies the number of wales or ribs, and the courses per inch.

Ticking - A striped cotton fabric, traditionally made of only black and white, but now comes in a wide variety of colors. It is used for covering mattresses or cushion pads, or can be made into curtains or shades.

Tricot - Usually made from nylon, this soft and thin fabric is made with crosswise elastic ribs in the back and non-elastic on top. It is seldom used for draperies due to its lack of body, but is beneficial for custom sheeting.

Tussah Silk - A raw, typically Indian silk, in a yellowish-brown color, difficult to dye.

V

Velour - (1) A term loosely applied to cut pile cloths in general, but also to fabrics with a fine, raised finish. (2) A cut pile cotton fabric comparable with cotton velvet but with a greater and denser pile. (3) A stable, high-grade woolen fabric which has a close, fine, dense, erect and even nap which provides a soft, pleasing hand.

Velvet - A warp pile cloth in which a succession of rows of short cut pile stand close together so as to give an even, uniform surface. When the pile is more than one-eighth of an inch high, the cloth is usually called Plus.

Viscose (Rayon) - The most ancient of man-made fibers. Well know for its distinctive sheen used in highlighting patterns and its ability to add luster and strength to cotton and silk blends.

Voile - A thin, open-mesh cloth made by a variation of plain weave. Most voiles are made of polyester. Similar to ninon, but with a much finer denier of yarn with a soft, drapable hand.

W

Warp - The yarns which run vertically or lengthwise in woven fabric.

Weft - The yarns which run horizontally in woven fabric.

Wool - An expensive versatile fabric which comes from the fleece of domesticated sheep. It has excellent insulating uses and is wrinkle and flame resistant.

Worsted - Fabric made of twisted yarn, of a wool type.

Textile Fibers and Their Properties

NATURAL FIBERS

COTTON
Drapability:	excellent hang, soft hand
Color fastness:	good, vat dyes best
Sun resistance:	excellent, sun does not rot
Abrasion resistance:	excellent
Sagging:	does not stretch, except when wet
Resiliency:	poor, packs easily, wrinkles easily, very absorbent, burns
Care:	wash or dry clean and iron at high temperature

Cotton generally wears excellently in drapery (print or plains).

LINEN OR FLAX
Drapability:	good hang, not as soft as cotton
Color fastness:	good to poor, prints do not hold their color as well as plain fabrics
Sun resistance:	excellent, sun does not rot
Abrasion resistance:	excellent
Sagging:	strong, does not stretch
Resiliency:	poor, packs badly, does wrinkle
Care:	dry clean and iron at high temperature

Linens are excellent in plain and casement fabric and good in prints.

SILK
Drapability:	good hang, medium to soft hand
Color fastness:	good
Sun resistance:	poor, rots in short time, lining helps
Abrasion resistance:	good
Sagging:	strong, does not sag
Resiliency:	good, does not pack badly
Care:	dry clean and iron at medium temperature

Silk is rarely used in drapery today due to sun rot and cost.

WOOL
Virtually unused as drapery fabric.

MAN-MADE

RAYON
Drapability:	good hang, soft hand
Color fastness:	good to excellent (solution dyed)
Sun resistance:	good, but not as good as cotton or linen
Abrasion resistance:	good, but not as good as cotton or nylon
Sagging:	poor, stretches in loose yarns, but OK in tightly woven fabrics
Resiliency:	good, does not pack, wrinkles less than cotton or linen
Care:	dry clean and iron at medium temperature

Rayon is blended with other fibers: cotton, acetate and linen.

ACETATE
Drapability:	good hand, soft hand
Color fastness:	good (solution dyed)
Sun resistance:	good, but not as good as cotton or linen
Abrasion resistance:	good, but not as good as cotton or nylon
Sagging:	poor, stretches in loose yarns, but OK in tightly woven fabrics
Resiliency:	good, does not pack, wrinkles less than cotton or linen
Care:	dry clean and iron at low temperature

Acetate blends well with other fibers, including rayon and nylon.

POLYESTER
Drapability:	excellent hang, very soft hand
Color fastness:	good to excellent
Sun resistance:	excellent
Abrasion resistance:	good, sheers must be handled with care. Fabric can be bruised.
Sagging:	excellent, does not stretch or shrink
Resiliency:	good to excellent, does not pack, wrinkle-free
Care:	wash or dry clean and iron at low temperature

Polyester is an excellent fabric for most drapery applications. It blends well with other fibers. In polyester cotton blends, the fabric will wrinkle less.

NYLON
Drapability:	good, soft to stiff hand, not as soft as polyesters
Color fastness:	good to excellent
Sun resistance:	poor
Abrasion resistance:	excellent
Sagging:	excellent, does not sag
Resiliency:	good to excellent, does not pack, wrinkle-free
Care:	dry clean and iron at low temperature

Nylon is not widely used in drapery fabric.

ACRYLIC
Drapability:	excellent, very soft hand
Color fastness:	excellent, if solution dyed
Sun resistance:	excellent, good as cotton or linen
Abrasion resistance:	good
Sagging:	very good, does not stretch
Resiliency:	very good, does not pack, wrinkle-free
Care:	dry clean and iron at low temperature, 50 degrees

Acrylic fabrics hang well and do not sag. Can be blended with polyester. Modacrylics are flame-resistant.

DYNEL
Drapability:	excellent, soft hand like acrylic
Color fastness:	excellent
Sun resistance:	good to excellent
Abrasion resistance:	excellent
Sagging:	excellent, compared to rayon or acetate
Resiliency:	very good, does not pack, wrinkle-free, low flammability
Care:	wash only, ironing does not affect it much, use low heat

DRAPERY FABRICS -
LOOK AND PERFORMANCE

Satins and Jacquards

Usually the most formal and traditional, they are generally made from tightly woven, heavy, soft material which hangs straight from top to bottom in (formal) folds.

Casements, Open Weaves

These have a lighter, more casual feel. They are usually made from loosely woven, textured yarns that hang in looser folds than the formal satins and Jacquards.

Sheers

Made of soft, see-through fabrics, sheers are appropriate in most decors. Light and airy, they are sometimes used in combination with heavier draperies in more formal settings. They are billowy unless weighted, and can be made to drape quite well.

Prints

Suitable in most decors, prints are made from a light, tightly woven fabric, usually cotton or cotton-polyester blends.

Drapery Linings

Linings add substantially to the luxurious appearance necessary for good window treatments, and also provide a fuller, pleated look for maintaining a soft, drapable hand. The lined look provides uniformity to the exterior appearance of a home, while offering a broad choice of textures, weaves, colors and patterns for the interior. Linings also help to extend the life of draperies by affording some protection against the sun. They also help protect draperies from water stains - either from condensation on the inside of the window or from a sudden shower. Insulated linings contribute to energy conservation, keeping homes cooler in the summer and warmer in the winter.

Fading

The combination of sunlight and air pollution will eventually take its toll on all colors. There is no such thing as an absolutely colorfast material or dye. Some colors however will show fading more dramatically than others. Bright colors tend to show fading more than subdued tones and solids will began fading before prints.

BIBLIOGRAPHY

Arched Window Solutions
Diane Deeds
1stBooks Library, 2000

Authentic Decor: The Domestic
Interior 1620-1920
Peter Thornton
Seven Dials, 2001

Beautiful Windows: Stylish
Solutions from Hunter Douglas
Window Fashions
Meredith Books, 2001

Caroline Wrey's Complete Curtain
Making Course
Overlook Press, 1997

Complete Book of Window
Treatments & Curtains:
Traditional & Innovative Ways to
Dress Up Your Windows
Carol Parks
Lark Books, 1995

Creative Curtainmaking
Made Easy
Heather Luke
Watson-Guptill, 2001

Creative Window Treatments
(Creating Your Home)
Betterway, 1996

The Curtain Book: A Sourcebook
for Distinctive Curtains, Drapes,
and Shades for Your Home
Caroline Clifton-Mogg, et al
Bulfinch Press, 1995

The Curtain Sketchbook 2
Wendy Baker
Randall International, 1999

Curtains
Creative Publishing International,
1998

Curtains: A Design Source Book
Caroline Clifton-Mogg
Ryland Peters & Small, 2001

Curtains and Draperies: History,
Design, Inspiration
Jenny Gibbs
Overlook Press, 1994

Curtains, Blinds & Valances (Sew
in a Weekend Series)
Editors at Eaglemoss
Betterway, 1998

Curtains, Draperies & Shades
The Editors of Southern Living
Sunset Publishing Company, 2000
Curtains for Beginners (Seams
Sew Easy)
Creative Publishing International,
1998

Design and Make Curtains
and Drapes
Heather Luke
Storey Books, 1996

Encyclopedia of Curtains:
Complete Curtain Maker
Catherine Merrick, et al
Randall International, 1996

Fabrications: Over 1000 Ways to
Decorate Your Home with Fabric
Katrin Cargill, et al
Little, Brown & Company, 1999

Great Window Treatments
Claire Martens
Sterling Publications, 1998

House Beautiful Windows
Sally Clark, et al
Hearst Books, 1997

How to Dress a Naked Window
Donna Babylon
Krause Publications, 1997

Ideas for Great
Window Treatments
Christine Barnes, et al
Sunset Publishing Company, 2000

Interiors: An Introduction
Karla J. Nielson, David A. Taylor
McGraw-Hill Higher Education,
1994

Judith Miller's Guide to Period-
Style Curtains and Soft
Furnishings
The Overlook Press, 2000

Low Sew Window Treatments
(Creative Textiles)
Creative Publishing International,
1997

Make It With Style:
Window Shades
Donna Lang, et al
Clarkson Potter, 1997

Make Your Own Curtains
& Blinds

Lani Van Reenen, et al
Storey Books, 1994

Making Curtains & Blinds
Dorothy Wood
Southwater, 2001
More Creative Window
Treatments: Complete step-by-
step instructions with full-color
photos for over 60 distinctive win-
dow treatments
Creative Publishing International,
2000

The New Draperies in the Low
Countries and England
Negley B. Harte
Oxford University Press, 1998

Sew a Beautiful Window:
Innovative Window Treatments
for Every Room in the House
Sally Cowan
Krause Publications, 2001

Sheer Style
Tessa Evelegh
Laurel Glen, 2000

Simply Window Treatments
Sunset Publishing Company, 1999

The Smart Approach to
Window Decor
Lynn Elliott, et al
Creative Homeowner Press, 2000

Southern Living Curtains,
Draperies & Shades
Sunset Publishing Company, 2000

Textile Fabrics and
Their Selection
Isabel Wingate
Prentice Hal, 1970

Two-Hour Window Treatments
Linda Durbano, et al
Sterling Publications, 2001

Practical Home Decorating:
Curtain and Shades
Melanie Paine
Reader's Digest Adult, 1997

A Portfolio of Window &
Window Treatment Ideas
Creative Publishing International,
1995

The Ultimate Curtain Book: A
Comprehensive Guide to Creating

Your Window Treatments
Isabella Forbes
Readers Digest, 2000

Victorian and Edwardian Décor
Jeremy Cooper
Abbeville Press, 1987

Victorian Interior Decoration
Roger W. Moss, Gail C. Winkler
Henry Holt, 1992

Victorian Style
Judith Miller and Martin Miller
Mitchell Beazley, 1993

What's in Style: Window
Treatments
Megan Connelly
Creative Homeowner Press, 2001

Window Decor
Susan E. Mickey
Sterling Publications, 2001

Window Dressing: From the
Editors of Vogue & Butterick
Butterick Company Inc, 2000

Window Style: Blinds Curtains
Screens Shutters
Mary Fox Linton
Bulfinch Press, 2000

Window Treatments
Linda Hallam
Better Homes & Gardens Books,
1997

Window Treatments (Singer
Sewing Reference Library)
Creative Publishing International,
1997

Windows: Beautiful Curtains,
Shades, & Blinds You Can Make
Meredith Books, 2001

Windows: How to Make Curtains
and Blinds (Inspirations)
Alison Jenkins
Southwater, 2001

Windows: Recipes & Ideas:
Simple Solutions for the Home
Richard Lowther, et al
Chronicle Books, 2000

Windows with Style: Do-it-your-
self Window Treatments
Creative Publishing International,
1997

INDEX

ACKNOWLEDGEMENTS

We would like to acknowledge the following designers whose exceptional work appears in the photographs in Dream Windows:

Alcorn Interior Design (pp 51BR, 174T)
B. Axel Interior Design (pp 55TR, 89TR/TB, 186BR, 191TR)
Rosa Bensky (pp 43TL/BL, 44T/B, 45T, 80, 86TL/TR, 136, 138BL, 141)
Chapman Design Group (pp 53BR, 54TR, 173ML)
Claire Grenier-Kennair (pp 115B, 168B, 170B)
Halina Catherine Design (front cover, pp 42, 84T/B, 85TR/B, 171BR)
Interiors by Lisa (pp 116T, 144T)
J.D. Design (pp 6, 7, 48B, 52BR, 54TL)
Joan Barrett Interior Design (pp 50BL, 51, 81T, 190B)
Claire Kennair (p 47T)
Carmen Kodric (pp 49T, 51BL, 86B, 116B, 126T, 130ML/MB, 137T/B, 145B, 171T, 172T, 186BL, 187BL)
Penny Niggemann Design (pp 83B, 109, 139, 173BL)
Mike Niven Interior Design (pp 52T, 53T/BL, 189MR)
Sharon Templeton (pp 43R, 47B, 48TL, 49B, 55TL, 55B, 82BR, 85TL, 88TR, 89T, 104, 105T, 106, 108T, 108T/BL, 110, 111T/B, 113T, 114B, 115T, 127, 128TL/BL, 129, 130TL/TR, 131, 132T/B, 133, 134T/BL/BR, 135, 138T/BR, 140, 143T/B, 144BL/BR, 145TL/TR, 146T, 147T/B, 170TL/BR, 172BL/BR, 174BR185, 186TL/TM, 187TL/MR/TR/BR, 188, 189TL/TR/ML/BL/BR, 190TL/TR, 191TL/ML/BL/BR)
Tom Flatt Interior Design (pp 45B, 50T/BR, 82T/BL, 83T, 87, 88B, 112, 146B, 152, 164-167, 171BL, 175T)
Sandra Tonietto (pp 2, 46B, 142B, 162-163)
Walli Neumann Design (pp 107, 117T, 175BR)

We would also like to thank the following photographers for their contributions:

Daniel Dutka (front cover, pp 42, 84T/B, 85TR/B)
Jac Jacobson (pp 52T, 53T/BL, 83B, 109, 139, 173BL, 189MR)
Michael Mahovolich (pp 82T/BL, 83T, 87, 112, 152)
Systems 4 Productions, Inc. (pp 2, 6-7, 42R, 43TL/BL, 44T/B, 45T, 46T/B, 47T/B, 48TL, 48B, 49B, 52BR, 54TL, 55TL, 55B, 80, 86TL/TR, 88TR, 89T, 104, 105T, 106, 108T, 108T/BL, 110, 111T, 113T, 114B, 115T/B, 129, 131, 132T/B, 133, 134T/BL, 135, 136, 138T, 138BL, 141, 142T, 142B, 143T/B, 145TL/TR, 147T, 162-163, 168B, 170TL/TR/B, 172BL/BR, 186TL/TM, 189TL/TR)

Grateful acknowledgement is also due to the following companies for their beautiful illustrations and photographs:

Bridgeman Art Library/Private Collection (pp 31BL, 34T, 40T)
Bridgeman Art Library/Mallett & Son Antiques Ltd., London, UK (p 25TL)
Shade-O-Matic, Canada (pp 154-160)

Lastly, we would like to thank the following artists for their immeasurable contributions to Dream Windows:

Patricia M. Howard (pp 10T, 11TL/TR/ML/MR/BR, 12ML/TR/BL, 13TR/BL, 14, 15TL/TR/MR/BR, 16, 17TR/BL, 18-24, 25BR, 26-27, 28TL/BL, 29-30, 31TL/TR/BR, 32-33, 34BR, 35TR/BR, 36-39, 41, 56-73, 90-103, 104MR/BR, 119ML/BL, 121T/B, 122M/B, 123, 125, 148-150, 151T/M, 177, 179B, 181M/MR, 220-226)
Carlotta Tormey (pp 10BL/BR, 11BL, 12BR, 13TL/BR, 15BL, 17TL/BR, 25BL, 28BR, 35ML, 79T, 194-219

*In the event of an error or omission, please contact Randall International.